IT ALL MATTERS

Why We Are the Way We Are

AL STROHMAYER

Cover Illustration by Jim Hunt
www.jimhunt.us

DEDICATION

For my wife; my love, my best friend, my typist, co-editor, and fonte Elaine, Mary, Marilyn, Konchalski, Ranalli, Hogan, Strohmayer; all one and the same, without whom this effort would still be on my "Maybe Someday" list.

For my Mom, who gave me life and passed along whatever gift for writing I have, and who, at a different time and place, might well have gained the recognition that passed her by.

For my children and their families in the hope that by baring my soul they will come to better know and understand me and, of more importance, begin the journey to a better understanding of themselves.

CONTENTS

Acknowledgements/ 6
Introduction/ 8

IN THE BEGINNING/ 9

Who's Pushing Me/ 10
The Dark Room/ 11
Thanks, Mom/ 12
Lost in Great Neck/ 13
Mr. Happy/ 14
Christmas 1944/ 15
1-2-3, 1-2-3/ 18
Oh, Come On/ 21
Christmas 1945/ 27
My Pal/ 30
Reaching Up/ 33
I'm Only Looking/ 35
Oops!/ 36
Getting Even/ 37
Mr. Anthony/ 39
Dear Little One/ 42
Too Young/ 45
It All Matters/ 48

THAT'S LIFE/ 50

Under the Influence/ 51
It Hurt So Bad/ 61
The Merger/ 65
Bye, Bye, Loneliness/ 67
The Flying Shell/ 69
Knock, Knock, Who's There?/ 70

CONTENTS CONT'D

The Lady in Green/ 72
The Pamphlet/ 74
Mensch – All/ 76
My Little Black Book/ 83
Foolish or Fooled/ 87
Defining Success/ 94

SUNSHINE/ 95

A Marriage Toast/ 96
"Checkbook" Janet/ 98
Now is Here/ 99
Promise Them Anything/ 105
Let it Snow/ 107
Ah, the Joy of Discovery/ 111
A Reasonable Guy/ 113
What Is This Thing Called Rap/ 115
The Bargain/ 117
The Predicament/ 118
The Last Laugh/ 120
The Visitation/ 122
Flog/ 124
Good Morning/ 129
Holiday Greetings/ 131
On Keeping It Simple/ 133
Help!/ 136
Casual and Comfortable/ 139
A Cry for Socialized Packaging/ 143
The Price You Pay/ 146
On Becoming a Recluse/ 148
Standing Tall/ 150
Whatever, Whenever/ 152

CONTENTS CONT'D

Rage/ 156
It's Moo Moo Time/ 162
Print Me/ 166
We Get Too Soon Old, Also Stupid/ 172
The Options are Limitless/ 176
Xmas Shopping for an Orangutan/ 180
It's Xmas Time Again/ 187
To Drive or to Fly/ 190
The Longest Day and Night/ 197
Comments Never Made/ 207

OH, MY GOD! / 209

Saying I Love You/ 210
About the Woman of My Life/ 213
Two for Scotch/ 214
A Birthday Wish for a 50-Year-Old Son/ 215
It's a Shame/ 217
By His Side/ 219
A Certain Feeling/ 222
Regret and Hope/ 223
Get up My Son/ 225
Another Letter – Another Son/ 230
Dear Son/ 232
On the Edge/ 233
In His Hands/ 245
About the Author/ 252

ACKNOWLEDGEMENTS

Many to thank for their encouragement, ideas, and assistance:

Joe and Ruth Accordino
Paul and Florence Bernbaum
Bill and Peg Cawthra
Marty and Sandy Daniels
Wash and Bobbie Dayton
Bob and Pam Ernst
Yvonne Gray
Bob Grote
Kate Helfrich
Brian and Sue Hogan
John and Jayne Hogan
Kevin and Pamela Hogan
Bob and Nancy Kenney
Tom and Pat Kenney
Pati Lewellyn
Paula Loomis
Bob and Jan Maloy
George McCaskey
Father Wilmot Merchant II
Florian and Betty Novovesky
John and Emma Ohnemus
The Pettes: Vin, Terese, Michael, Daniel
Mike and Julie Porcelli
Jim and Barbara Pringle
Bob and Terry Regan
Gary and Evelyn Sessi
Steven Schmidt
Robby Sternberg
Ken and Wendy Strohmayer

ACKNOWLEDGEMENTS

A special thanks to Jim Hunt, www.jimhunt.us, who illustrated the cover and took the time and had the patience to answer the most basic of questions.

To Yvonne Gray, editor and consultant, who spent a good portion of her life correcting my grammar and disproving the theory that a comma is a cure-all.

To Bob and Jan Maloy, new friends who never stopped showing interest or giving encouragement. Many Thanks.

To George McCaskey, former actor, television performer, and present day Corinthian, who dared to criticize and who made me aware of the importance of awareness.

To Sandy Daniels, dear friend, who first read the nearly completed manuscript, who offered encouragement and suggestions, who corrected spelling errors and relocated many misplaced commas, I extend my gratitude along with the promise that, should there ever be another book, she once again will be blessed with a first reading opportunity.
How's that for showing gratitude?

And of course there is my wife, Elaine, my greatest supporter who gave of her time, who set new boundaries for patience, who typed every word, and retyped most every other word. I owe her big time and love her even more.

And to all those who, in a senior moment, I may have failed to mention, I ask forgiveness; memory is the first to go.

INTRODUCTION

Many have described life as a journey.
I believe that.

It is my purpose in writing *It All Matters* to show how all
happenings, all experiences, all people, somehow and to some
extent affect the traveler and therefore the journey, and how a
faith in God makes easier man's journey through life by
providing both spiritual strength and peace of mind.

I have also heard that every person is capable of writing one
book.
May the following words serve to support that belief.

PART 1

IN THE BEGINNING

When first impressions are made.

When everyone needs a Mom.

WHO'S PUSHING ME?

The year was 1937 and I was all of three.
My Mom, my older brother, and I were on our way to
       Europe to visit mother's parents.
I don't know if we were on the Queen Mary or what,
       but pictures make it quite clear that we were
       on one large boat, probably an ocean liner.
I see this kid, this child, standing on the deck wearing this
       silly little tam and coat that no longer fit him.
That's definitely not a smile on his face.
It's a pout that clearly expresses some kind of
       annoyance, a condition, so I've been told,
       not uncommon to this three-year-old.
Anyway, as the story goes, the ocean was rougher than
       usual that day, and little Derfla, that's me, the
       three-year-old, couldn't understand why he had trouble
       standing and walking on the deck.
His comment, nicely complementing the pout on his face was,
       "Who's pushing me?"

I guess you'd have to be there to appreciate it,
       but I must say, as the years passed and I
       struggled to understand myself,
       that same question was never far from my thoughts:

       "Who's pushing me?"

Time and events would eventually change this to

       "Who's rocking my boat?"

THE DARK ROOM

I must have been six or so.
The memory has never left me.
My folks would dine out frequently with friends,
  and my brother and I, with no say in the matter,
  would accompany them.
After dinner, it was off to someone's house for coffee,
  cake, and cards.
There was no TV then, and so it was up to my brother
  and me to entertain ourselves.
I still vaguely recall the room.
I remember it was dark and the bed was covered with coats.
Someone had given me a harmonica, and I found this dark,
  out-of-the-way room a perfect place
  to begin my musical career.
And so I did.
I played the harmonica and I danced, or tried to.
Lost in my imagination and free of all inhibitions,
  I was center stage.
That is until I happened to glance at the now
  opened door to see what seemed like a
  thousand smiling, laughing, cheering faces.
I think I died a little at that moment.
I know it ended any thoughts of a musical career.
When I got home, I gave the harmonica to my brother,
  who was still laughing at the time.
Maybe I threw it at him.

THANKS, MOM

Two blond-haired boys, seven and ten, kneeled before a bed and
    prayed.
Their mother stood beside them teaching the words.
The prayer was in German, which my brother and I could neither
    speak nor understand.
And so we memorized the words.

Seventy years later I am able to recall only a few, "Lieber Gott,"
    and "Himmlische Ruhe." "Lieber Gott" is easy to translate;
    it means "Dear God."
I didn't need a dictionary for that, but I did need one for the other
    words: "Himmlische Ruhe," meaning heavenly peace.
I wish I could call my brother for the other words, as he was three
    years older and remembered them far longer than I.
As an adult, he would on occasion recite the prayer.
Sadly, he passed away more than a decade ago and took the words
    with him.

I believe Mom's prayer was one of love and family, of heaven and
    peace, for those feelings were always with her.
For my brother and me, the words served as both an introduction
    to prayer and to the Lord.
God became real, and now through prayer we were able to
    reach Him.

Thanks, Mom.

LOST IN GREAT NECK

I cannot recall the year or exactly how old I was,
      but I do recall the experience.
In fact, I relive it every time I see an ice cream cone.

We were visiting my uncle in Great Neck, New York.
It was a picnic and we had finished our barbecue.
My request for ice cream was answered with a shiny
      quarter and directions to a nearby ice cream parlor.
It wasn't far, and I had no problem getting there.
And so with ice cream in hand, I headed back,
      or at least so I thought.
What should have been a left turn became a right and,
      what should have been a five minute walk in
      the right direction, became a marathon run
      in the wrong direction.
It wasn't long before tears would flow,
      and the ice cream would melt, and Derfla,
      that's me, would suffer his first anxiety attack.
To this day, I recall the terror of being lost.
Even now as an adult, I will go to great lengths to avoid
      the unsettling, out-of-control feeling of being lost.
 It is an experience I choose not to relive.

Oh yes, Mom and Dad rescued me that day.
They had taken their car, realized my error and found me.
After drying away the tears and assuring me that I was safe and
      that all was well with the world, they bought me
      another ice cream cone.
But you know, it didn't taste as good.
It never would.

MR. HAPPY

It was 1944.

I was ten years old and, like most ten years olds, I loved Christmas.

It was a happy time, a time of giving and receiving, and for me as a
      ten-year-old, it was mostly a time of receiving, and what could
      be better than that?

Well, there is one thing that could have been better, a lot better:
      not having to play the piano at Christmas time for
      family and friends.

Mom arranged things. It was all her doing; she selected the songs
      to be played and then made sure my brother and I were
      prepared.

I could only play one song, "The Maiden's Prayer."

It must have been the name that attracted me.

That's the only reason why now, after some sixty plus years,
      I can still recall its name.

The composer had to be a genius, not for his ability to write music,
      but for his ability to entitle it.

My brother would share the spotlight by playing the violin as poorly as
      I played the piano.

Together we made everyone look forward to New Year's Eve.

I think the applause given was more a celebration of closure than
      accomplishment.

When friends started to arrive later and later in the evening,
      Mom realized my brother and I were not concert bound
      and accordingly turned her efforts and or
      attention to something entirely different --- poetry.

You got it: Mom would write, and my brother and I would recite.

While I now appreciate Mom's efforts, I certainly didn't then.
      Picture it if you will:
      a young lad who loved and lived sports having to first
      memorize and then recite a poem of considerable length
      before what seemed like the entire neighborhood.

It was enough to have me pass on Christmas.

Mom's poem of 1944 is found below.
It's really quite good, a lot better than it used to be.
I can almost forget the pain of reciting it.

CHRISTMAS 1944

Christmas time year after year.
Is to me a great event.
I figure out three months ahead.
Just how much money I should spend.

And when you come to think it over
At what really is at stake,
You always reach the same conclusion,
It's just a game of give and take.

I chiseled here and cut down there
And must admit quite frankly,
Tough going for a guy like me
Who gets a quarter weekly.

But with the tactics that I use
I'm sure there's little doubt,
That with the exchange of presents
I take in far more than I give out.

With the calendar I kept for months
I marked the days gone bye.
Now it is here and I am glad.
You know the reason why.

A kid like me lives in the present
In real carefree joyous style.
And only Christmas time with all its splendor
Can make the waiting worthwhile.

Now look at Dad; he seems content
There in the chair that stood the test.

It All Matters

And may it always bring to him
The well deserved nightly rest.

With minerals and plants and insects, too
My brother Walt seems delighted
But not for me Santa.
Those things don't get me the least excited.

There is no reason why a fellow
Should sit and analyze it all,
When there is so much more excitement
In just a baseball bat and ball.

Let that be all for now;
The party's still in full swing.
Time to take a look around
To see if anyone else came in.

Did I forget the most important?
That's just like me, how true.
A "MERRY CHRISTMAS" from happy me
to all of you.

It must have been this time in my life that I acquired the nickname of
    Mr. Happy.

Much later as a parent with enough children to form a choir,
    I attempted to pass on the custom of children performing
    at Christmas time.
I mean, it could have been anything: song, dance, poetry. I would have
    accepted off-color jokes or animal imitations, anything,
    just something.
It was not to be.
With little support from my wife, who was not seeking revenge
    as I may well have been, and with a reception of utter disdain
    from our six slackers, the issue was dropped, dashed, diced,
    buried, and forgotten.

It All Matters

Or so I thought. As if called to action by history, or possibly my
       Mom, our grandchildren would revive the custom by
       performing a song, a dance, a recital, a prayer.
There is one major difference:
       our grandchildren actually enjoy performing.
You can see the joy in their faces. They love performing.
And I love them for their efforts.
And I admire them for their attitude.
I'm sure my Mom would agree.

1 – 2 – 3, 1 – 2 – 3, 1 – 2 – 3

There were always girls.
I just hadn't noticed them.
And then, as if by magic, those silly little things
      that dressed and talked funny and
      played with dolls rather than sports
      suddenly became a factor in my life.
I don't want to say I found myself attracted to them,
      not yet anyway; that would come later.
For now, let's just say I became interested.
Like overnight, those silly little things became
      cute little things with magical little bumps.

I guess my first adventure came when a neighborhood girl
      asked me to accompany her to a party.
I think she did it on a dare, and I accepted on a dare,
      probably my brother's.
It was a long walk to the party, and
      talking did not come easily.
I mean, how do you talk to a girl?
The party was held in an apartment house, and
      there were a lot of kids there.
The boys were on one side of the room,
      the girls on the other.
That is until some genius, probably a girl, thought
      it would be fun to play "spin the bottle."
Little did I know that I was about to get my first kiss
      from an obviously love-starved teenager.
No, it wasn't my date.
It was some girl named Beverly with big, hungry lips.
WOW! Mom never kissed me like that, I thought,
      as I rushed back to the bottle for seconds.
The walk home didn't seem very long at all.

Soon after my first kissing adventure, I found myself
      challenged by my first dance, the Junior High Prom.

It All Matters

Armed with the memory of a first kiss and the thought of
      holding a girl, I decided to give it a try.
There was only one problem: I couldn't dance, not a lick,
      never interested, just another one of those
      silly little things that suddenly wasn't so silly.
I mean, how do you go to a prom if you can't dance?

Good "ole" Mom came to the rescue, or at least she tried to.
Explaining my dilemma to her, she mercifully offered
      to teach me.

1 – 2 – 3, 1 – 2 – 3, 1 – 2 – 3
God, is this what one had to do to hold a girl?
I thought seriously of developing a high fever,
      but I was committed, and so I went.
Mom wouldn't have it any other way.
God, the girls looked pretty and so grown up;
      their bumps seemed to have grown overnight.
I really liked this one girl, Georgia.
She had blond hair and a bubbly personality,
      which, by the way, always attracted me, even though
      it never led to anything but trouble.
And so gathering my courage, I walked over to where the
      girls were giggling and asked Georgia for a dance.

1 – 2 – 3, 1 – 2 – 3, 1 – 2 – 3
I could see she wasn't thrilled, and so I made the first
      serious mistake of my courting, dancing, dating days.
I asked Georgia if her boyfriend, some guy named Tommy,
      whom I had replaced as the Blue Devil's shortstop,
      could dance better than I.
Without a second's hesitation, Georgia replied,
      "Oh yes, Tommy's a really good dancer."
It was like being slapped with a wet towel.
Later, I watched them dance together and had to admit
      that Tommy was a lot better dancer than
      he was a shortstop.
I had seen enough.

It was time to go home.
Maybe there was an easier way to get to hold a girl.
Either that or I needed more dancing lessons,
        and this time, I vowed, it would be from
        someone who never heard of Strauss or

1 – 2 – 3, 1 – 2 – 3, 1 – 2 – 3
Sorry, Mom.

OH, COME ON

He was my father.

He came to the United States at the age of nineteen in 1923 from a
small town in the Black Forest of Germany.

Dad was the last of eleven children, never knew his father, who passed
away at an early age and rarely saw his mother who, with her
children, ran a mineral water business during the first
World War.

He would talk about selling bottles to the soldiers on the train and the
soldier-like helmet he wore while doing so.

Wearing the helmet was no doubt an early indication of a future
businessman.

Like so many others, he immigrated to the United States seeking
opportunity, freedom, and, yes, prosperity.

In those days, one had to have a sponsor to enter this country and
become a citizen.

Patience was also required, patience to wait one's turn.

Dad's sponsor was his sister, who had come to the United States years
before and who lived in Great Neck, NY, with her husband
and children.

Dad always had patience and so he waited his turn and, after many
months, came to view the Statue of Liberty for himself.

He arrived with little money, fewer contacts, and a high school
education that provided just enough English to get by.

I was always grateful I never heard him roll his Rs or confuse his
Ts with Zs, as many German immigrants did.

Must have been mother's influence; she never would have tolerated
a rolling R or a Z for a T.

Anyway, he made due, and using what came naturally – versatility,
adaptability, cajolery, and charm he tackled a great variety
of jobs.

His first job here was delivering ice to affluent homes on Long Island.

It was in so doing that he met his wife to be, my mother to be, who at
the time was employed as a governess for one of the
"wealthies" on his ice route.

An interrupted courtship would begin.

With a background in math, he would soon hook up with
    H. R. Grace & Co in the accounting department.

Then using a combination of charm, guile, and whatever else he could
    find or borrow, and with just enough Spanish to be
    understood, he secured a job with Grace Line, Inc., in of all
    places – Lima, Peru, as of all things, a plantation supervisor.

That's how he described the job anyway.

All I know from pictures is that he rode around the plantation on a
    horse, even though he had never been on one before.

With that as a background, how could I not believe his often repeated
    "senorita on the woodpile" story?

It was here then, in the city of Lima, Peru, that the expression,
    "Have Line will Travel" was born.

Mom wasn't adverse to traveling either, as she would fly to Lima
    where they would wed and where my brother would be born.

Either boredom, or a stomach ailment, or both would drive them all
    back to the States where the Great Depression awaited them.

Like many others, Dad struggled to provide for his family.

As the story goes, confirmed by Mom, he had on occasion
    run some booze between New York and New Jersey using his
    own car for transportation and his wife and son for cover.

I'm sure, that had I been born in time, I also would have been an
    accomplice.

Whenever questioned regarding his transgression, Dad would
    invariably reply,
    "You gotta do what you gotta to do." And he did – always.

He had other expressions, some more original, which we'll cover in
    detail later.

Conditions improved in the late '30s, and Dad found a job as a
    salesman for a major New York beer producer.

Five years later, he would become that area's district manager.

The second World War would bring new opportunity, and he would
    leave the security he had for the bar and grill business.

Before this chapter of his life would end, he would own and run
    several.

And the money rolled in, and the good times began: summer camp for
 the boys, cruises for my parents, and vacation trips for us all.
The "booze" business would also make possible college education
 for both my brother and me.
After the war when business slowed down, Dad would sell his
 business and return to selling beer.
A promised return to management never materialized, and so
 disappointed, he would, with a friend of many years, return to
 the bar and grill business.
By now, Dad was approaching seventy, and his friend and partner was
 even older.
Neither the business nor the relationship faired well, and, after a few
 struggling years, the business was sold.
Two part-time jobs would mark the last of Dad's ventures: one as a
 greeter for a famous steak house on Long Island, the other as a
 security guard checking luggage at New York's
 La Guardia airport.
The man would try anything and probably did at one time or another.
 My knowledge is limited to what I was told and the little
 I personally witnessed.

Think what you will, my father was a provider, chasing money all his
 life and enjoying every step along the way.
That much I'm sure of.

I never remember Dad staying out overnight.
In fact, I never remember him missing one of Mom's dinners or the
 one or two cocktails, make that two or three, that preceded
 dinner.
I also recall his after dinner cigar and his favorite chair to which he
 retreated and the ashes that frequently fell.

Mom, always seeking to maintain order, would invariably come to the
 rescue; removing the cigar from his lips, the ashes wherever
 they fell, and planting a kiss on her husband's lips.
Dad loved to play cards, pinoccle and rummy his favorites, and,
 whenever possible, he would play for money.
He also loved to play the ponies, and, when in business for himself,

he would spend many an afternoon at the Jamaica or Belmont
racetracks.

Scotch and beer were his favorite drinks, and he was not a stranger
to either.
A good scotch, a good meal, and a good cigar, in that order, and he
was a happy man.
He might also throw in a good beer with the good meal.
Whenever he approached our apartment building he would always,
and I mean always, beep his horn to his own special tune.
If I could write music, I would do it now.
To Mom, it was a signal to finish preparing dinner.
For my brother and me, it meant we'd eat in thirty minutes. It was a
happy time.

Dad's favorite sports were soccer and baseball.
On Sundays during the fall and winter, with me at his side, he would
watch the local German-American soccer team.
TV and the summer would lead to baseball and he became a loyal,
if not well informed, Yankee fan.
In our youth, he would take my brother and me to Yankee games.
Later, when retired, he would frequently spend afternoons at
Yankee Stadium by himself.

After the war, many Saturday nights were devoted to putting together
CARE packages of coffee, sugar, flour, cigarettes, and other
unavailables for Dad's family abroad
I still see them there at the dining room table filling package after
package, Dad with his cigar and beer, Mom with her lists.
When they made their first visit over there after the war, a good
portion of the town welcomed them at the railroad station.
Understand, a good showing by the family alone could account for a
good portion of the town.
 Nevertheless, the recognition must have made them proud.

If you haven't picked it up by now, know for sure that he *lived*,
this father of mine; he enjoyed life to the fullest and made sure
he missed very little of it.

I loved him for that and always wished I could have been more
      like him.
But unfortunately, you don't get to choose your genes, and I found
      myself quite naturally following in my mother's image: shy,
      serious, conscientious, and always saving and putting money
      aside and, worst of all, postponing fun for tomorrow.

Most revealing about my father were his favorite expressions.
Unique in that they rarely were appropriate.
Unique most of all because of their overuse.
It was unusual for a day to pass without hearing at least one of them.
His favorite and most commonly used expression was,
                **** "Oh, Come On."
When he disagreed with someone, or when his thoughts ran contrary
      to someone else's, he could invariably begin his disagreement
      with,
                **** "Oh, Come On."
And wouldn't you know, our kids would remember him for that; I like
      to believe as a tribute.
To this day some twenty years after his passing, they can frequently be
      heard saying,
                **** "Oh, Come On."
And they say it his way with emphasis on the "Oh," then a short
      pause, and then a final equally emphatic, "Come On."
I say it too, and without fail my thoughts go to him.

Dad had another expression, not as socially acceptable as
      "Oh, Come On," but probably more meaningful.
He would use it when "Oh, Come On" didn't adequately express his
      objection.
It was, I'm sorry to say, " — You!"
Again, it was said a certain way, his way, with a rolling emphasis on
      the nasty part, and the "you" following along naturally.
Again, I wish I could describe it as well as I remember it.
Just know that it was an overused group of words expressed uniquely.
This was a natural for the boys to pick up, and they did, despite my
      continued efforts to discourage its use.
I took solace in the fact that again they did it his way, ending it in a

smile, as if they were remembering him and paying tribute to a man who did it his way, who lived his life as he wished, and spoke as he saw fit.

And I guess that's not so bad in these days of repressed feelings, cover ups, insecurity, and non-commitment.
As I said, I wish I were more like him.
Oh well, someone has to "hold the fort."
Someone has to worry and save and plan for tomorrow.

I can just hear Dad's reply to that last statement,
        **** "Oh, Come On."
Or, at least I sincerely hope that would be his choice of favorite expressions.

It was toward the end of World War II.
I was eleven years old and had come home to find my mother in tears.
I had never seen her cry like that before.
Between sobs she told me that her parents,
she called them Mutte and Papa,
had been killed in an air raid
and that there was nothing left of them or theirs.

A few months later Mom wrote the following:
(I am both happy and proud to share it with you.)

CHRISTMAS 1945

The winter sky looks bright and festive,
And stars are glistening far and wide.
Christmas is here and up to heaven
Rise tender tunes of "Silent Night."

The children live in great excitement.
Their hearts beat at a rapid pace.
And grownups drop their daily worries,
A smile creeps on a tired face.

The year went fast since last we gathered
Beneath the spray of mistletoe.
The wheel of fortune just keeps on spinning,
Thus months will pass and years will go.

What is a year, 'tis just a book
On which we fondly look.
And turned down pages, noting days
Dimly recalled through memory's haze.

And tearstained pages too, that tell
Of starless nights and mournful dwell.
The laugh, the tear, the light, the shade,
All 'tween the covers gently laid.

No leaves uncut, no page unscanned,
Close it and put it in God's hand.
Then let the peace that Christmas brings
Enter your heart on silent wings.

Just look about and see the splendor.
We're rich today for from above
Flowed down a priceless gift.
Christmas brought us unselfish love.

We need this love when war and suffering
Has left its mark on helpless prey.
It's love alone that heals and comforts,
Makes old hearts young and young hearts gay.

And wounds and hearts are healed much faster
If love applies its magic touch.
And all you need is understanding,
It costs so little, does so much.

So when the tree has lost its splendor,
And gifts and toys are tucked away.
Let us make sure that love and kindness
Are still with us, have come to stay.

So that next year when we open
The book of life, our glance will fall
Upon the page that bears the message,
"Christmas has come, has come for all."

This from a woman who came to this country by herself in 1923.
She came with a limited knowledge of English, little money,
        and a sponsor she had never met.
She was nineteen years of age.
She was my Mom, and I've always been awed by her sense of
        adventure.

And proud I will always be.
Proud of her courage and determination.
Proud of how she accepted heartache and turned it to love.
Proud she was my Mom.

I close with her words of love, for she said them so well, and they
        meant so much to her:

            "So when the tree has lost its splendor,
            And gifts and toys are tucked away,
            Let us make sure that love and kindness
            Are still with us, have come to stay."

MY PAL

He was larger than life.
I had heard that, but you know you had to see it to believe it.
Well, I saw it, or rather him, and he was larger than life.
Of course, I was only nine years old, very impressionable,
      and already a die-hard Yankee fan.

Our family was vacationing in Greenwood Lake, NJ.
The hotel where we stayed was on the lake and featured its own
      boat dock, restaurant, and bar.
On this "day of days," I was on the dock fishing with bread balls-
      that's right, bread balls.
Someone must have convinced me that that was the best bait to use.
      It was probably my brother, who didn't want me to catch
      anything.
As I said, I was only nine and very impressionable.
The dock was well below the level of the hotel, requiring more than
      a few descending steps to reach.
So there I was fishing when something caught my attention, a move,
      probably footsteps.
I turned and all I could see was some shoes, some fancy two-toned
      shoes descending the steps.
White pants soon followed and then what grabbed my eye was the
      man's size. In every direction he was huge, not big, but huge.
The "giant" approached and his face finally became visible.
My God, it was Babe Ruth!
There was no mistaking him.
There before me stood the greatest baseball player of all time.
And he actually spoke to me.
In a deep, husky voice he said,
      "How you doin' kid?"
I remember that, I really do.
What I don't remember is what happened next.
Family had watched the event unfold from the landing above, hiding
      behind whatever they could find.

It All Matters

They had asked the Babe to "make my day," and, as he had for so
      many other kids, he obliged.

Anyway, I was told that I literally swooned, dropped my bread baited
      fishing pole, and came perilously close to falling in the lake.
I don't remember any of that.
When you're in a coma, thoughts are difficult to recall.
Nor do I remember having a picture taken with the Babe and my
      brother.
But we did, and I have proudly displayed that same picture for some
      sixty years now.
And, oh yes, on a return trip to the hotel, Babe autographed the
      picture.
As I later learned, he regularly frequented many of the bars in the area,
      and this one at the Greenwood Lake Hotel was one of his
      favorites.
I just happened to be at the right place at the right time.
Next to when I met my wife, I consider this summer day at
      Greenwood Lake to be the luckiest day of my life.
I had to say that because my wife will eventually read this.
And memories are memories, but "you gotta do what you gotta do."

A few years later when playing in the Babe Ruth League,
      our team found itself short of Louisville Slugger bats.
It was during the war years, and shortages of all kind were common.
I had combed the area with little success.
My father suggested I write to my buddy, the Babe.
And so I did.
And you know, he answered me, making a few suggestions and
      signing the letter, "Your pal, Babe Ruth."
I carried that folded letter in my wallet for years, showing it off
      whenever possible.
Only when the writing began to fade was it removed, framed,
      and positioned next to the autographed picture.

I saw Babe Ruth for the last time in the mid '40s, when he made
      one of his last appearances at Yankee Stadium.
I couldn't believe it was my pal.

A camel coat hung loosely over his stooped shoulders
   doing little to hide his frailty.
His voice was but a whisper, barely audible.
I wasn't the only one crying.

The greatest ball player of all time died of cancer on
   August 16, 1948.
His body lay for viewing at the main entrance to Yankee Stadium
   the next evening.
My father asked me if I wanted to go and say goodbye.
I couldn't do it; I didn't want to see him like that.
I wanted to remember him as he was, my bigger-than-life pal.

REACHING UP

I studied hard in high school.
It must have been in an effort to outdo my brother and gain my
      father's approval.
No matter, I studied and studied, and in my junior year I found myself
      placed in an English honors class.
Some reward!!
I really didn't need or want that.
These kids were different.
Today, you'd probably call them nerds. Most all wore glasses,
      most all had large heads, and either they looked like a draft
      would blow them over or a hurricane wouldn't.
I, on the other hand, was perfect – didn't wear glasses
      and had an athlete's body, except for my feet
      and head which were slightly flat.
Most bothersome about my new classmates was that
      I had to refer to a dictionary to understand them.
This proved somewhat awkward when trying to converse,
      and I found myself relying more and more on "yes"
      and "no" nods.

Anyway, things were moving along OK.
I kept up with the prescribed readings and held my own in class.
I did that by hiding and saying as little as possible.

And then the first bomb dropped.
We were studying poetry at the time, or at least the others were,
      and as a home assignment, teacher gave us a poem to write,
      any subject we wanted.
Like that mattered!
Like choice of subject would make it doable.
I mean, how many athletes do you know who write poetry or
      even know what it is?
After an award-winning plea to my mother, I managed to convince
      her to write it for me.
Tears work wonders on mothers.

She was into poetry and wrote the thing in a few minutes.
The subject was totally feminine, something about flowers.
I didn't care; I got a good grade, and poetry was now history.

There was little time to celebrate, as our next assignment was to
      memorize a meaningful incident from a book and recite it to
      the class without notes, without assistance of any kind
      – just get up in front of the class and make an ass of yourself.
The only thing I felt confident about was that I would do just that.
And this time there was no Mom to bail me out.
I was on my own in some very deep "doo–doo."
Since we could select from the book of our choice, I chose something
      I thought would be exciting and therefore easy to memorize.
There was this American ace pilot in World War II, Captain Eddie
      Rickenbaker.
He and his crew were shot down in the Pacific, and part of the book
      devoted itself to their struggle to survive on a raft surrounded
      by sharks, with little water or food to sustain them.
The part I selected to memorize and present featured that moment on
      the raft when a seagull landed on the head of our hero,
      Eddie Rickenbaker.
Here, I said with trembling voice, was food, if only he could catch it.
Eddie, slowly, carefully reached up for the bird and—
      I still don't remember what happened.
I know I froze, blushed a scarlet red, and shamefully retreated back to
      my desk where I prayed for admission to any other world.

This time it was the teacher who came to my rescue saying she
      particularly appreciated the mysterious ending, since it would
      surely encourage others to read the book.
I could have kissed Bella then (that was her name). It must have been
      her whiskers that stopped me.

The fear of public speaking never left me entirely, even though later
      on it would become a job requirement.
I would always think back to Eddie and that dumb bird.
I hope you got him, Eddie.

I'M ONLY LOOKING

You might say I was an unhappy teenager.
You might also say I was a miserable teenager.
No doubt, those around me at the time would agree to both, with the
      exception perhaps of my Mom, who invented "mother love."

Guess I should begin with my early teens, when I involuntarily
      acquired a taste for soap.
Soap was mother's cure-all for swearing, and the nastier the word,
      the more soap she would apply.
Apparently it didn't do much to deter me, for it got so I could tell
      one soap from another.
About this time I began my career as a shoplifter.
You see, I had this friend, Bob, a real cool guy.
One day during lunch recess, "Mr. Cool" gave me a tour of the local
      department store and showed me how easy it was to acquire
      freebies.
This went on long enough for me to acquire quite a collection
      of yo-yos.
Unfortunately, big brother was watching, noticed my expanding
      collection, and mentioned it to Mom, who immediately began
      the "Great Inquisition."
Rather than have to endure another soap session, I confessed,
      and my career as a shoplifter came to an abrupt end.
It didn't take long for the "inquisitor" to take me by the hand and
      drag me back to the source of my collection.
Under her unyielding guidance, I returned the "fruits" of my pilfering,
      sheepishly explaining that I had forgotten to pay for them.
I remember the sales lady smiled, and my mother smiled, and
      I wanted to die.

Afterwards, whenever Mom would see my eyes wandering, she would
      give me that "don't even think about it" look, to which
        I would invariably reply, "Mother I'm only looking."
Years later, we would laugh about it. She was a good Mom.

OOPS!

Then there was the time I threw a baseball through my bedroom
window, which would seem to indicate an emotional
imbalance of sorts.

But, you have to understand, I was a Yankee fan, a real Yankee fan,
a devout, die-hard, out-of-your-mind, Yankee fan.

And so, as the Yankees went, so went I.

On this particular evening the Yanks lost 1-0 to the Red Sox in extra
innings, and my favorite rookie pitcher, Spec Shea, took
the loss.

He had pitched brilliantly, shutting out the Red Sox in their own
ballpark for nine innings, and then in the bottom of the tenth,
he gave up a home run, losing both his shutout and the game.

And that same baseball that I had been tenderly tossing up and down
for nine innings suddenly went flying through my bedroom
window.

"Accidents will happen," I explained to my folks.

Amazingly, they bought the story, rationalizing that no child of theirs
would deliberately throw a baseball through his own window,
someone else's perhaps, but not his own.

My folks were never die-hard Yankee fans, and so they couldn't
understand the necessity of fully venting after a
heartbreaking loss.

Had they been such, they would have known that what occurred was
no accident, and the incident therefore would have cost me far
more than a few weeks of allowance.

Good fortune is not always deserved.

GETTING EVEN

Roddy was my age and a real milquetoast.
Neither very strong nor fast afoot, he was easy prey and soon
       became the scapegoat of my frustrations.
At last I could play "big brother" and give the orders.
And give the orders, I did.
And tease and take advantage, I did.
And pummel Roddy whenever I pleased, I did.
Not surprisingly, it wasn't long before Roddy disappeared.
Although we lived in the same apartment building, suddenly he was
       nowhere to be found.
I figured he was hiding.
And then one day, when I was leaving the building, I saw Roddy
       up ahead.
I yelled for him to wait up for me.
He chose to run.
It took a few blocks to catch him, but I did, and of course he had
       to be punished.
But somehow, I couldn't do it.
I think deep down I was afraid I was losing my scapegoat, and so
       I was friendly and played nice guy.
"Hey buddy, where you been? I've been looking all over for you."
       We parted without incident, but I guess it came too late, for a
       few weeks later Roddy got even with his bully companion.
I was in the lobby of the local movie theater waiting for the next show
       to begin.
Out of nowhere came this brute of a kid, who first greeted me by
       name and then proceeded to pummel me to my knees.
He parted with the words, "That's from Roddy."
To this day I think he was a "hit" man.
OK, a "hit" boy.

I never saw Roddy again.
He successfully hid from me until he moved to California.
I guess he figured that was far enough away.
I figured that I got what I deserved; a bully usually does.

Not a good memory for me, but a good learning experience.
And should I ever see Roddy again, I'd like to believe that I would
    find a way to apologize.
I'm pretty sure I would also ask for the name of his "hit" man.
He was good, and you never know when you might need a little
assistance.

MR. ANTHONY

It seemed as though there was always my big brother Walt, the nicest
   guy in the world.
Trouble is, it took me a while to realize it, like most of my terrible
   teens.
You see, on the one hand there was Walt: wise beyond his years, good
   looking, charming, personable, and if that weren't enough, he
   was three years older and the first born, which to the second
   born made him the favorite.
And there I was: a foot shorter, distant, distraught, with a terrible
   temper, and knowledge limited to an imaginative variety of
   curse words, all subject to release upon the slightest
   provocation.
Now add the fact that Walt was the family's Mr. Anthony.
For you youngsters, Mr. Anthony had his own radio show in the '40s,
   where he solved other people's problems – the audience
   would call in, and Mr. Anthony would offer a solution to their
   problem.
How's that for a comparison?
I mean, how do you make your presence known?
How do you gain recognition?

My first choice of action was rebellion – temper tantrums, throwing
   things, cursing, crying, bullying, shoplifting, and I even gave
   some serious thought to running away.
Fortunately, there was also a practical side to me, and running away
   cancelled out Mom's cooking and a comfortable bed –
   option rejected.
The bottom came for me when by chance I overheard my parents and
   Mr. Anthony discussing the possibility of sending me away to
   military school.
That did have an effect.
You might even say it scared the hell out of me.
It is truly amazing how quickly one can grow up when confronted
   with an alternative life style that represents the last thing in the
   world desired.

And so grow up I did, realizing at last that there wasn't too much to
    be gained from rebelling.
A more productive course of action would come later when I became
    aware that "Mr. Perfect" was not so perfect after all, that there
    were actually things I could do better than him:
- Walt was a "B" student, so I locked myself in my room and
    studied and studied and became an "A" student.
- Walt was an average athlete, and so I drove myself to excel
    and became better than him in most sports, and I was three
    years younger. It felt, Oh, so good!
    Hey, look at me!
It took awhile, many talks, and a letter of concern, but Walt would
    eventually come to realize that his little "pain in the ass"
    brother had something worthwhile going for him,
    something he could admire and even be proud of.

It's funny how things work out.
Who would have thought that this "terrible teen" would grow up
    and gain the acceptance he so long sought from his family.
And who could have ever imagined that his big brother would become
    his best friend, his counselor, his guiding hand,
    his Mr. Anthony?
And that they would come to respect and love each other, as brothers
    should.

Only death could interfere, as my brother would pass away at age 53.
He had problems even he couldn't resolve, and didn't know how to
    share with others.
I died a little with him.
I will always miss him.
In my fantasy world, I had imagined us as old men, enjoying the
    winter of our lives together, laughing at the past
    and welcoming the future.
It was not to be.
I will always regret that I never thought enough to help him, that
    I wasn't there for him as he had been for me.
But then he never asked for help.

How could he?
He was Mr. Anthony.
He was here to help others.
That had always been his role.
He would accept no other.

I believe Walt is with God now, doing the same thing he did on earth,
        helping others, that he has just changed locations.
"Auf Wiedersehen," big brother.
I shall always look up to you.

I was sixteen and a junior in high school when I received my brother's
letter.

Walt was nineteen and a sophomore in college when he wrote it.

Parental and brotherly concern had risen from the fact that at this
time Derfla, that's me, had found little time for anything
but studies.

Nothing could lure me away from my books until I was satisfied that
the lesson had been learned, the assignment completed, and I
was in control.

I recall one day in particular. It was the weekend and my folks and
brother were going to the track. They pleaded with me to join
them, but I had some unfinished work to complete and
declined the offer. To keep them happy I placed a $2.00
bet with them, picking the first numbers that came to mind;
as in the number five horse in the second race. Hours later
they returned and handed me a twenty-dollar bill. I had won.

The next day Dad asked me to pick another horse. I think he believed
he had found a way to win. Anyway, I picked, and he lost,
and he never asked me again.

Below is my brother's letter, his plea to me for normalcy. I keep the
letter in an album with other important papers:

New Brunswick, N. J.
Oct. 17, 1950

DEAR LITTLE ONE,

I think the time has about arrived when a tip from an older brother
should be considered seriously.

The average family is confronted with many problems, most of which
concern the younger members.

Our family is no exception; I certainly presented problems at times
which worried Mom and Dad very much, but we managed
to work something out.

You are no different!

I don't think our intelligence is that contrasting that our grades in
school differ that much.

I graduated with an 85 average, and you will probably
terminate your high school career with a cumulative average
very close to 90.

Although five percentage points can mean a lot, I don't think that
either of us was gifted with an extremely fertile mind.

You are obtaining your marks by driving yourself. I don't even know
whether you're finding time to read this letter.

I studied at times, and I can't deny it, not that there is any reason for
denial. But I didn't whip and punish myself by imprisoning
myself in my room from morning till night.

You are, without a doubt, ruining your own health and endangering
those of others.

Didn't you ever have the feeling that you wished you could do
something besides study, when you know very well you
should study?

One of these times, do what you feel like doing and just do briefly the
work that is requested.

Once in awhile just brush your books aside; they won't shoot you!

I don't want you to become a dead-head or a "party-poop."

Studies aren't what make you nice to be with.

Develop a personality and then a vocabulary.

Build a love for life and then study why, how, and when we lived it.

Learn to be patient and polite and then reap the rewards.

Your brother,
Walt

Now, some fifty-seven years later, I look back on my brother's letter
and come to the conclusion that, while his intentions were no
doubt sincere, his observations were to some degree short on
fact and long on opinion:

- Yes, I agree there was little difference in our intelligence, but
there was, I believe, quite a difference in the results of our
efforts: Walt graduated with an 85 average in the middle-top
half of his class, while I graduated with honors, ninth in my
class and a 92 average.

- No doubt, I studied to an extreme, far more than he had, and probably more than I should have, but come on, how else does one with average intelligence graduate 9th in a class of 235. (I looked up the class size.)

- To me, the only health endangered was possibly my own, and I saw no danger in exercising whatever brain matter I was either blessed or shortchanged with. Although, I must admit, that if the situation had been reversed and Walt was the one cooped up in his room studying out loud with great intensity, I, too, would have been concerned.

- And yes, I frequently felt like doing something other than studying, but what he didn't understand was that behind my overly zealous effort was the goal of doing something better than him, something besides sports, something that would bring me recognition, even approval from Mom and Dad.

- One other thing: I didn't worry about being "Mr. Popular," or "developing a personality," or "being nice to be with," for there was no way I could have competed with him at that level where he enjoyed his greatest strengths.

Whatever the differences of opinion, and however I struggled to negate my brother's comments and/or suggestions, know that his words did reach and affect me.

Of greater importance, I would in time come to recognize and appreciate this loving, caring, big brother, who made the effort to help his "pain in the ass, little one," an effort far different than mine had been, an effort whose nature and direction was unknown to me.

TOO YOUNG

I must have been sixteen or seventeen when I realized she was not just
    another girl.
She was special and was to become my first girl friend.
By that, I mean that Bonnie was the first girl I felt comfortable with
    and whose company I enjoyed.
She was several years younger than I, and that probably made me
    immature, but that's the way it was.
It wasn't something you thought about.
It was only about how you felt, and I felt good about Bonnie.
We lived in the same apartment building, she on the first floor,
    I on the fifth.
I don't know if it was because I spent a lot of time waiting for the
    elevator that was already there, or because Bonnie spent a lot
    of time watching to see who was at the elevator, but that's
    where we would frequently "bump" into each other.
I remember once I was in my room and heard a whistle.
It was Bonnie out back pushing a baby carriage.
She asked me to join her, and I did, and we went for a walk.
I must say it felt good.
Oh, a little strange with her baby sister in the carriage, but good.
In those few short years, we never kissed.
It was just a good feeling we shared.

And so when I went off to college, joined a fraternity, and needed a
    date for my first stay-over weekend party, meaning the girls
    stayed over and the boys moved out, I naturally thought of
    and invited Bonnie.
She was too young to attend, and I was too immature to realize it.
Her mother, however, realized both and rightly said "NO" to the idea.
In the next few years I would rarely see Bonnie, as I would become
    more involved in college activities, and yes, girls.
Then as a junior on a rare visit home, there was a knock on our door,
    and who would come dancing through but Bonnie in her high
    school prom dress.
A quick hello, a revealing twirl or two, and she was gone.

My God, she looked good, all grown up.
But I did nothing.
Surprised and confused, I let the moment pass, telling myself I was,
    after all, seriously involved with someone else.

And then as a senior and now pinned to that same "someone else,"
    I yielded to the past and on another trip home, called Bonnie
    and asked her for a date.
Well, I had to be sure, didn't I?
We went to a movie, "Gone With The Wind."
It was also our last date.
Perhaps I expected too much.
Perhaps I should have taken more initiative.
Anyway, nothing happened, not even a good night kiss.
We held hands in the movie, but that was all of it.
I drove her home, she said goodnight and was out of the car before
    it stopped.
She might just as well have said good-bye.

Now as I look back on those days, I cannot help but feel that my first
    stay-over party weekend was a turning point in my life, for my
    substitute date for that same weekend was the same
    "someone else" I would later pin; and who, after graduation,
    would become my wife and the mother of my first
    two sons.
She would go on to divorce me some ten years later taking
    the boys with her and breaking my heart.
So much for substitutes.

But God is good, and in time He would send me the love of my life,
    Elaine, who for thirty-eight years now has given me more love
    than any man is entitled to.
We met at a Parents Without Partners dinner.
Our first date was the movie "Yours, Mine, and Ours," and it
    must have impressed us, for our families would soon unite,
    and my two sons would become five, and a daughter would
    bring the total to half a dozen.

It All Matters

Well, it wasn't easy, but it was good, and it was right, and to this day
    we share a family love that grows stronger with each passing
    year.
God is indeed good.

I will always remember Bonnie as she was as a teenager.
I wonder how she is now and how her life has worked out.
It must be true, that you never forget your first girlfriend.

A FEW MEMORIES, A FEW IMPRESSIONS, ALL LEFT BEHIND BY WHAT WAS THEN. ALL TO AFFECT WHAT WHAT WAS YET TO COME.

- I still feel unsettled when someone or something "rocks my boat."
  I prefer the steady course with as little change as possible.

- I still feel unsettled whenever I get lost, for getting lost means losing control.
  And to this day, I prefer eating ice cream out of a dish.

- Playing a musical instrument of any kind is out of the question; that would mean performing and overcoming inhibitions, --- and I just know someone would be watching.

- Whenever my attitude is poor, which is frequently, I try to recall my grandchildren joyfully performing at Christmas time, and what a difference a good attitude can make.
  It helps even, "Mr. Happy."

- To this day, I remain a die-hard Yankee fan and now share those same feelings with my five sons. As for the Babe, he'll always be the "greatest," and always my pal.

- I'd rather clean a garage than dance; it's a lot easier and I don't have to concern myself with comparisons.

- Whenever I give a talk, my "insurance policy" is right there with me. That would be my notes.
  No notes – no talk – no more "dumb" birds.

- As a senior citizen, I try not to swear, but it happens, and when it does, I swear I can taste soap.
  I don't collect yo-yos anymore, and when i go shopping I feel Mom is watching, and more often than not, I'll hear myself say, "Mother, I'm only looking."

- Now, whenever I watch a Yankee game, I remove all hard objects from the viewing area and surround myself with cushions.
  Not to take a chance, my wife has had our windows treated for missile impact.

- Today, whenever I see a bully, I think of my relationship with Roddy, and I feel both regret and thankfulness; regret because I bullied a friend, thankfulness because that same friend taught me a lesson.

- I will always cherish my brother's memory, and while I'll never be a Mr. Anthony, I do try. Six children have made that effort necessary.

- And once in a while, I think back to my adolescence and Bonnie and what might have been. And then I think of my first marriage and what was. And every day I thank God for my life with Elaine.

It all matters.
We are all molded by people and events.
Everything that happens has an affect.
And so, if by chance, you don't understand yourself and
      you don't understand why you are the way you are,
      take the time to reflect on your past.
All the answers are there waiting for you.
It may not be the easiest thing you ever attempted, but it just
      might be the most rewarding.

PART II

THAT'S LIFE

Lasting impressions leave their mark.

When you realize there is no tooth fairy.

UNDER THE INFLUENCE

If anyone ever needed a life-style change, a personality lift, a
 broadening of horizons, it was I.
Four years of high school saw me develop little more than an aptitude
 for studying, and more self-discipline than anyone would ever
 need or want.
Put it this way: I was cautious, conservative, and controlled, also
 reluctant, reticent, and reclusive.
Self-conscious would also fit.
Girls and organized sports were definite goals, but I was only eighteen
 and still sucking my thumb.
Got the picture? If it's not clear yet, perhaps this will help; I thought
 socializing was a political party.
With all that going for me, I left for the college of my choice,
 Rutgers University of New Jersey, where my brother Walt was
 a senior and also a Fiji, that is, a brother of Phi Gamma Delta
 fraternity.
High grades and Walt's influence had much to do with my acceptance
 to Rutgers.
His influence had everything to do with my becoming a Fiji.
You see, Walt was obliging, caring, and both fun and people-loving.
Add to that a marvelous dry wit, and you have a charmer.
That last word, "charmer," says it all. That's what he was.
I think the brotherhood assumed I would echo his personality.
What they failed to realize was that this wasn't the Alps, and my
 brother couldn't yodel.
Anyway, my freshman year went fast.
I lived in a dorm, continued my obsession with studies, giving my
 life to calculus and thus ending any thoughts of becoming
 an engineer.
If that wasn't a sign of change and things to come, then certainly the
 beginning of a social life was. Pledging to a fraternity,
 in addition to doing what pledges do, also brought me in
 contact with a wide variety of guys, some of whom would
 become and remain life-long friends.

51

This is really about them, those special few guys, and how they
      introduced me to a life-style change, a personality lift, and yes,
      a broadening of horizons.
As my sophomore year began, brother Walt entered the army and I
      entered the Fiji house.
Walt wasn't too happy with the arrangements, but I was.
My roommates were Joe Heinen, Bob Howard, and Vint Gwinn.
They would become part of the "special few."

Joe was a best buddy throughout college, and we kept in touch for
      fifty years thereafter.
He came to Rutgers from University Heights, Ohio.
Physically, he looked like he came off a farm – tall, blond, broad-
      shouldered and strong, with a mid-western accent.
It wasn't long before he was renamed Jess.
Jess had a very dry sense of humor, and we would frequently
      exchange barbs.
I guess you enjoy someone who makes you laugh, and I enjoyed Jess.
Nothing seemed to bother him. He just went with the tide and
      enjoyed himself along the way.
I was fortunate in being his friend and socializing with him.
And socialize we did – Broadway shows, Village jazz,
      holidays with my folks on Long Island, and more double
      dates than I can remember.
We would room together again our senior year.
He was the same Jess, never changed, never would change, always
      relaxed, always obliging, always good company, always ready
      and able to share a new experience.
And thus he introduced me to a different way of life.
The exposure was enlightening, and I would like to believe some of it
      rubbed off on me. A little would have been a lot.
Thanks, Jess.

And who could forget Bob Howard out of Newburgh, New York?
Like, who could forget a tornado?
We used to call him Hub, as he was relatively short and unrealistically
      wide to the point of appearing square.
His thickness brought him great strength and balance. It also brought

a neck that challenged measurement.

Hub wrestled intramurally his freshman year, pinning a bear in
thirty seconds.

We knew then he was special.

But his love was football, and football he played: freshman and
varsity, making First Team All East and Honorable Mention
All American.

Hub was dynamic, sometimes temperamental, and outspoken,
on occasion critical of others, and always and most of all,
competitive.

I always said it was best to be on Hub's side regardless of the issue.

Just once I challenged that philosophy.

Fortunately, the good Lord was watching over me.

It was a simple dispute. We had many over nothing important.

He probably criticized something I held dear, like my hairstyle, which
featured a series of carefully coifed waves and which required
my entire adolescence to develop.

One word lead to another, and I challenged him physically.

Remember, I was only a sophomore and struggling for intelligence,
for had Bob accepted my challenge, someone else would be
writing this.

As I recall, Jess just sat there shaking his head, as if to say,
"I don't want to see this."

Perhaps Bob saw him and realized he wanted no part of a
manslaughter charge.

Walking away from the situation was probably the nicest thing
Bob ever did for me.

He just turned and left. I don't know who was more relieved, Jess or I.

Another similar incident occurred during our senior year.

I was big on attending class, Bob was not, and so he would frequently
borrow my notes.

On this particular day, he criticized my note taking, claiming he had
trouble reading it.

Not taking too kindly to his comments, I loudly suggested he borrow
someone else's.

Hub just stared at me, the veins in his eighteen-inch neck pulsating.

This time, not counting on the Lord or luck, I turned and left.

Wisdom is a wonderful thing.

Other than these two incidents, and a few dozen more, we got along
fine. We even double-dated a few times.

The fact that I had the only car in our class, a 1938 kelly green
Dodge Coupe, might have had something to do with our
commradery.

Anyway, on this particular date, I had dropped off my honey bunny,
passionately kissing her sealed mouth goodnight, and headed
back to the fraternity with Bob and his date in the rear.

I don't know what they were doing back there, but it definitely was
something mother never taught me.

I had read a lot about noisy lovers, but this was closest I had ever
come to hearing one. Make that two.

It was almost animalistic. It was animalistic.

Perhaps, I thought, my love life was lacking in certain ways.

Oh, to be so free, so natural, so uninhibited, so loud.

I'd have to work on that, all of that.

Thanks Hub. You were a real eye opener.

Vint Gwinn of St. Marys, West Virginia, nicknamed Ginder, was not
my closest friend, nor for that matter, was he anyone else's.

You see, Vint was too busy achieving success, leaving little time for
developing relationships.

Vint's record at school was embarrassing, not for him, but for anyone
who wanted to compare accomplishments.

Here are a few of Vint's:

- President Senior Class
- Vice President Student Council
- Member of numerous honorary societies to include
  Who's Who and Cap & Skull
- Member of Phi Beta Kappa, elite honorary society
- Henry Rutgers Scholar
- Dean's List – four years

Add to that freshman and three years of varsity baseball. Also notable,
if only to me, was that it was thru Vint's encouragement that
I tried out for and made the same freshman and varsity baseball
teams. I didn't play much, but I always had a good seat.

Nothing was unattainable for the Ginder, and he conveyed that
       positive attitude to anyone who observed, or worked,
       or lived with him.
He was a model of consistency, always striving, always accomplishing,
       always succeeding – an "A" student, an "A" athlete, an "A"
       at anything he pursued. Vint was certainly someone to
       emulate, someone special who constantly reminded others
       through his actions that the number one reason
       for going to college was not to have a good time.
We roomed together again our senior year along with Jess.
The two were so different. Jess so relaxed you had to remind yourself
       he wasn't sleeping, and Vint ever on the go, ever straining to
       accomplish his goals.
The only question with Vint was how high he would climb, how
       successful he would be.
Jess, Hub, and Vint all with different approaches: Jess always easy,
       Hub always competing, Vint ever striving.
All successful in their own way.

And then there were the Kenney twins, Tom and Bob, from
       Elizabeth, New Jersey.
No one or two would effect me more positively.
For what they offered was unique in its completeness – a love of life,
       a respect for others, a desire to succeed, and an ever present
       sense of humor.
Yet their love for each other would surpass all else.
Not once in four years of college, or on any occasion in the fifty years
       following, did I hear either one criticize the other.
They were and are today as brothers should be.
What makes their relationship so remarkable is the handicap they
       overcame, and I say "they" because what affected one also
       affected the other.
If either Tom or Bob experienced any kind of problem, or for
       that matter success, you could sense the concern or joy
       in the other.
It was like they were one.

Perhaps the past might help to explain.

      When Tom was a young lad he contracted polio.

      The disease stole the strength from his legs and put him on
      crutches, or as Tom preferred to call them, "sticks."

      Using them was how he got around, and get around he did.

      With love and encouragement from his parents and brother Bob,
      Tom not only overcame his handicap, I believe he used it to his
      advantage. What started as a handicap became a challenge and
      then an accomplishment.

There was very little Tom didn't try and even less he couldn't do. I'm
      talking bowling and fishing, and commanding his own boat.
      I'm talking golfing and swimming, pool or ocean. He could
      toss a football or baseball, or shoot a basket. I never saw him
      dance, but that wouldn't have surprised me either.

I played golf with Tom once at our 45th college reunion.

He beat me. Now I don't pretend to be a good golfer, but I'm not bad
      either, and he beat me. He'd prop himself up with one arm,
      and swing with the other. The ball would invariably sail down
      the middle of the fairway. I might add that it was not a warm
      feeling that I had for him as I looked for my ball in
      the woods.

Tom drove his own car with the assistance of hand controls.

He helped raise a family, two girls and a boy, all great kids,
      all successful in life.

He also helped a company, traveling the country as a Group Director
      of Human Resources for Becton Dickerson. At Rutgers, he
      was known, appreciated, and admired by anyone who had their
      eyes and heart open.

He served as president of Phi Gamma Delta his senior year, and not
      the least bit surprising, served as the coxswain for the
      freshman, junior, and varsity crews.

What is surprising is that he did not partake in track and field events,
      or on second thought, perhaps I just missed it.

Occasionally our families would join together for a week's vacation at
      the New Jersey shore.

It All Matters

My kids had only heard about Tom, but had yet to meet him.

So when Tom entered our cottage that summer day, they couldn't take their eyes off of him.

After introducing himself and chatting awhile, Tom left using a different door.

A few minutes later Bob entered using the same door Tom had used to enter.

Two steps in and Bob jumps up, clicks his heels, and exclaims, "I'm feeling much better now, must be the salt air."

To this day my now adult kids still remember and talk about the "miracle" at the Jersey shore.

It was on one of these vacations that I recall Tom struggling through the beach sand to reach the ocean's edge.

Once there, he wasted a little time selecting a suitable wave and diving in. I still hear his laughter as the ocean tossed him around.

Always there, always on the watch, was brother Bob, who, after Tom indicated he had had enough, would bring his brother's "sticks" to him, and Tom would fight the waves and struggle until he could stand.

And then, wouldn't you know it, the two would walk off laughing.

So many memories.

One day at Rutgers after leaving class, Tom, Bob, and I headed back to the frat house.

It had snowed the previous evening, and the walkway had turned to ice.

Not surprisingly, Tom slipped and went down hard.

I mean hard. I mean he lay flat on his back.

Instinctively, I reached down to help.

Bad move, because before I knew it, Bob had blocked my intentions placing a straight arm across my chest.

He then started laughing and chiding Tom for his clumsiness.

Then Tom started laughing and picked himself up with no help from anyone. That was always the message: Tom could do it himself.

They laughed all the way to the frat house.

I could do no more than follow along and marvel at the experience.

It All Matters

Memories are made of this. Special people are made of this.

In case you've missed it, the Kenneys are special people: Tom, the
         "biggest" guy I ever met, and Bob, the "nicest."
If I have placed Bob in the background, it is intentional, as I know he
         would have wanted it that way.
Bob has lived his life that way, always there when needed, always
         supportive, always encouraging, and most remarkably,
         always doing so without wanting to be noticed.
         A very special guy, indeed.
His school record included the presidency of one honorary
         association, and membership in others.
Bob also played freshman and three years of varsity lacrosse.
Later he would definitely be noticed in business, rising to the
         presidency of Elizabeth Town and Gas.
You might also say he was noticed at home, fathering and helping
         to raise three daughters.
Bob, the quiet leader with his own approach, and his own success.

All different, all with a different approach to life.
All successful in their own way.
For me they were all teachers, mentors, all providing me with a basis
         from which to grow.
I am ever so grateful to them, and all the better for having known
         them and having been their friend.

EPILOGUE

Vint's life and pursuit of success ended prematurely.

    Following graduation from Rutgers, he earned his Doctorate
at Princeton University.

    Then came LSU and a professorship there.

    On this particular field trip he was supervising some students at an
archaeological find. The earth suddenly gave way, suffocating him
and tragically ending all he had worked so hard to achieve.

    Vint is survived by his wife and family.

    He is remembered by all who watched his star rise.

Hub fell to a fatal heart attack at an age far too young.

    He was in his early sixties, serving as Manager of Training for
Pratt and Whitney.

    He is survived by his wife, son, and daughter.

    I'm sure Hub gave it all he had to the very end. He knew
no other way.

Jess and I got involved in a foolish battle of prides.

    I planned on visiting him on a recent trip south and called to make
arrangements. He said he had something going on and couldn't
make it. Not until I heard of his passing away several months later
did I understand. When I had called Jess he was already battling
complications from emphysema, feeling and looking poorly. And
as I also learned later, he wasn't seeing anyone, even his own
daughters. I should have known better. I knew he was sick, and I
knew Jess, and I should have put the two together. Instead, I
tripped over my pride and never called back.

    I shall always regret it.

Jess was little more than 70 when he passed away. He had devoted his career to the family business, the Heinen chain of supermarkets located throughout the Cleveland area. Jess had worked his way up through the organization and at the end was serving on the board of directors.
He is survived by his wife and family.
I greatly miss him.

Tom and Bob Kenney are still conquering life's challenges with a smile and a laugh.
They are both retired, living on or near the Jersey shore and enjoying life and their expanded families. Winters find them and their wives celebrating the warmth of Naples, Florida. We see each other too infrequently.

IT HURT SO BAD

She was bubbly, and silly, and fun to be with, and she had nice legs.
She was everything I wasn't, or didn't have.
Although I must say, my legs were kind of nice too, perhaps a little
      hairy and slightly bowlegged, but nice.
We were opposites, as opposite as Yin and Yang, or if you will, as
      opposite as battery terminals, each thinking they represented
      the positive side.
What one had little of, the other had in depth, and what the other had
      in depth, was sorely lacking in the other.
It was a natural setting for mutual attraction, and mutually attract
      we did.
We would meet at a basketball game my freshman year in college.
      It might have been her bubbly personality, or her silly remarks,
      and certainly her legs gave me something to think about. For
      sure my terminal was charged, and I was turned on.
The very next day there was a knock on my dorm room door,
      and there she was with her blond ponytail and her nice legs.
      It was the beginning of a four-year relationship, leading to a
      post-graduate marriage, and ending some ten years later in
      divorce.

As with most newlyweds, we had our share of problems: two years of
      military life, separation from family and friends, numerous
      moves, limited income, and two kids thirteen months apart,
      all serving as introductions to the realities of life. They also
      served to bring on the inevitable clash of opposite
      personalities, of different goals, and contrasting life styles.
And clash we did. Those same characteristics that once attracted, now
      separated and irritated.
In vain, we tried to change each other.
I, looking for a "stay at home" mom and house frau, and my wife
      seeking freedom and her own interpretation of self-fulfillment.
You see, this gal with the ponytail, nice legs, and fun loving
      disposition was also a talented dancer, the recipient of a
      scholarship to the Julliard School of Music in New York City,

which she would reject for marriage and family.
A choice, I believe, she would come to regret.
With self-expression dominating her thoughts, she would turn to
reading the "classics" of the time, such as Dr. Spock's work
on child rearing.[*]
One day I would come home to find the boy's room crayoned in a
rainbow of colors. I'm talking walls and doors and furniture
and closet space. Somehow the ceiling was overlooked. I'm
talking two days home from work: one for cleaning with a type
of acid, the other for recovering from a type of acid poisoning.
Wife explained it all as a wonderful experience in self-expression.
I rather explained it as the act of an irresponsible loon.

Unhappy with my analysis, she then directed her reading towards
works relating to personal growth and self-fulfillment.
I recall one such book was, *I'm OK-You're OK*,[*] which she,
I believe, interpreted as, I'm OK, you're OK, if I can do
as I want.

It was also at this time that a religious element came into play: and I
might misuse the word "religious," as it wasn't a church we
attended, but rather a fellowship, and, as I was to quickly learn,
there is quite a difference between the two.
Whatever, it echoed wife's newfound philosophy.
One day, I came home from work and noticed what appeared to be a
letter on our message board.
It really wasn't a letter. It was a poem, a love poem written to my wife
from another self-expressionist.
I guess he just acted freely as his heart dictated.
And so did I, as I found a new "home" for "Romeo's" poem. It was
under the sink in a can.
As for my wife, she seemed as pleased as I was annoyed.
But, I was also confused and concerned and determined to do
whatever I could to save our marriage.
I was also naïve, slow to learn, stubborn, and stupid, and in an effort
to show an understanding of her need for self-fulfillment,

---

[*] Baby and Child Care by Dr. Benjamin Spock
[*] "I'm OK-You're OK" by Thomas A. Harris

It All Matters

I bought her a car.

It wasn't the newest or biggest car in town, but it ran, and we hardly
could afford it.

As things turned out, it would be the same car she would leave in,
taking along our kids, and her and their personal belongings.

That day, that evening, was the bleakest, the darkest day of my life.

I will always remember the sight of their empty room and their empty
bunk beds.

That bubbly, silly, fun-loving gal with the nice gams had succeeded in
breaking my heart.

A six-month trial separation was the best I could do to delay the
inevitable.

During that period, I would attend my boys little league ball games
and then take them out for a bite to eat.

They would also be with me on weekends, when we would significantly
boost the count on the Mac Donald's burgers sold sign.

I would add to my list of naïve, stupid moves by attending a Sunday
gathering of her clique, knowing she would be there, hoping it
would show my willingness to compromise, to show I wanted
her back. What I did not expect was that she would be sitting
there next to her poet admirer. I felt so stupid. I felt even
more so when our eyes met, and I realized we were strangers.

Whatever remaining hope for reconciliation was dashed
when wife and kids moved in with yet another "free" spirit.

Referring to her new mate in one of our last conversations, she said,
"He makes me feel like a woman."

I do so wish that, instead of receiving her remark with paralysis,
I would have been able to reply with something entirely
appropriate such as, "Tell me, does he also fly and wear a
cape, and does he change his clothes in a phone booth?"

She got me good, that silly blond, with the fun-loving disposition.

"Should haves" count for nothing.

Shortly after the trial separation, wife took her pony tail, and nice legs
and flew to Juarez, Mexico, where she bought her freedom
using, not surprisingly, irreconcilable differences as the
reason for divorce.

Well, she got that part right, anyway.

The following months were as bleak and difficult as I can remember.

I threw myself into my work, slept on a cot in the spare room, had the
kids on weekends, all while struggling to keep the house, and
making child support and alimony payments.

But it was the boys who suffered most; divorce will do that to
children.

It will tear them apart, cause them to question their self-worth,
and in the end damage their self-confidence.

Repeated moves and school changes, and monetary problems would
all add to their confusion and insecurity.

I could see their hurt. I could feel the happiness when they arrived,
the sadness when they had to leave.

And so, when career opportunities would present themselves,
I would pass.

The offers would have meant moving many states away.

Not an easy decision to make, but the right one.

Right for me was being there for my boys.

Right for them was a stable environment, which I believed had to
include me. And so I stayed.

My work would keep me busy, but it would not satisfy the growing
loneliness that I felt.

A neighbor had told me about an organization called Parents
Without Partners where the lonely could meet others
in a similar situation.

I was ready and willing, and although as nervous as I can ever
remember, I went.

And it was there on my first visit to Parents Without Partners, my first
social venture since the separation, that I met the love of my
life, my future wife of now some 38 years, Elaine.

This was no attraction of opposites.

This was two people who knew who they were and what they wanted
both for themselves and for their children.

THE MERGER

It was my first date with Elaine.

Appropriately, although I didn't realize its significance at the time, the
movie's name was, "Yours, Mine, and Ours."

Had it been "Yours and Mine," it would have been even more
appropriate, as there was no room for "Ours".

When I drove her home that night, she invited me in.

I never did question invitations like that, so I gladly, eagerly, and with
great expectations, accepted.

What greeted me were the Hogans:

Terese, age five, Brian, seven, and John, ten.

Kevin, age thirteen, was there, yet he wasn't.

Feeling weak, I sat down as quickly as I could.

It wasn't long before Terese was on my lap, John was holding my
hand, and Brian was running the course of the second floor
landing yelling, "We have a father. We have a father."

With Kevin, the eldest, it was a different story.

He stayed in the bathroom the entire length of my visit.

And only on subsequent visits to the Hogans would he emerge,
realizing there was more to life then he could find in the
bathroom.

He would go on to test me with both a football and a sparring match.

I guess I passed, because he spent less time in the bathroom.

Don't misunderstand. His time there remained lengthy and a favorite
topic of conversation, although no one even once
volunteered to join him and solve the mystery.

The visits would increase in the months to come, and the families
would spend more and more time together – Elaine's four and
my two, Chris and Ken, ages eight and seven.

Within a year, Elaine and I would wed, and the four and two would
become six.

Please understand that a merger of this nature and size requires an
extreme condition of loneliness.

Both Elaine and I met that requirement.

Perhaps I more than Elaine, as I would only see Chris and Ken once
during the week for a ballgame and a bite to eat, and then on
weekends, when they would stay over. They were my only
company.

Elaine, on the other hand, had all the "company" she could handle
with the four Hogans for seven days a week.

What was missing for both Elaine and me was adult companionship
and its fringe benefits.

A cure-all wedding date was set, and shortly thereafter at a business
convention, I announced to a former business manager of
mine my intension to marry a girl with four kids.

He just shook his head, took a deep breath, and walked away.

I couldn't help but wonder if this business associate of mine
exemplified the meaning of a new word I had recently
learned.

The word was, "SCHMUCK.."

It's a New York word.

I looked it up. At best it means jerk or fool.

He was both.

BYE, BYE LONELINESS, HELLO SOMETHING ELSE

What followed was a period of adjustment for all.
Brian explained it best when he said,
"Kenny's my age and we're brothers, but we're not related."
Regrets were never mine, as the rewards were many. Confusion, yes,
    frustration, anger, in need of psychological help, yes, but
    never regret.
I took it as my responsibility to set an example, a good example, and
    what really happened in trying to help raise six kids, was that in
    the process, I grew up myself.
Daily challenges will do that. They will mature you fast and lead you
    to conclude that combining two families is about as easy as
    having a rational conversation with a teenager.
Petty jealousies abound, and all the difficulties of children growing up
    become exaggerated by both the situation and the sheer
    numbers.
No, it wasn't easy, and it wasn't an overnight struggle, but when you
    have a wife who tirelessly gives of herself and offers a love that
    has no bounds, you can "climb the highest mountain," you
    can do anything.
Well the years passed and to quote Kevin, "we all made it," the four
    and two, and I happily add to that list Elaine and I; we also
    made it.
They, the kids, are all grown up now.
Most all have homes and families of their own and yes, life's
    challenges to face and overcome.
But they persist as if following lessons previously taught.
Effort and hard work have brought them success, a success they
    thoroughly enjoy and freely use to celebrate life.
And best of all, they are their own best friends and socialize regularly.
Who could ask for more? Elaine and I have indeed been blessed.
God is good, and although sometimes it might take awhile to realize,
    He is good all the time.
All we need is a little patience and a lot of faith.

EPILOGUE

Kevin's lengthy stays in the bathroom continue to this day, and
    although no one has yet to spend time in there with him, some
    new and revealing information has come to light that leads to
    at least one assumption.
The new, revealing information is that on a special area next to his
    "throne" there sits a great variety of reading materials: a book,
    several magazines, the daily newspaper open to the sports page,
    an assortment of business related E-mails, and some unpaid bills.
    All this was accompanied by a set of reading glasses and several
    coasters, suitable for either a hot or cold beverage. There was also
    a plate holding a few remaining scraps of meat. I think it was
    steak, but it was so mangled I couldn't be sure.
The solution to the mystery came hard and fast;
    To Kevin the bathroom is his sanctuary ---- no disturbances, peace
    and quiet, and most all the pleasures ---- his safe house.
Of course there still remains the mystery of the shower;
    thirty minutes is a long time to shower and you have to wonder
    what exactly is in there to hold his interest.
    I'm almost afraid to look.
    Actually, I am afraid to look.
    Some things are best left unknown.

THE FLYING SHELL

It was our wedding dinner.
The newlyweds were trying to figure out a reason to celebrate.
I had just married a gal with four kids.
Elaine had just married a guy with two kids.
A lot of people just shook their heads in wonder.
Others walked away. Still others promised to pray for us.
Not our best man and matron of honor, Alan and Janet.
They were with us to celebrate, especially Alan.
He seized the moment and ordered the house specialty, stuffed
       lobster. It wasn't stuffed for long.
In fact, it wasn't anything for long.
Shells filled the air. People found themselves ducking to avoid injury.
       One lady ignored the onslaught and paid the price, as a rather
       large red missile found its mark, landing on the top of her
       elegantly coiffered hair.
I remember the three of us were embarrassed: Janet, Elaine, and I.
Not Alan. He just kept on shelling.
While we were not asked to leave, I have to believe the proprietor
       and his patrons gave a sigh of relief when we did.

KNOCK, KNOCK, WHO'S THERE?

I couldn't sleep. Wife lay next to me doing just that, but I couldn't
sleep.

The day had been as most others, filled with the stress and strain that
accompanies the merging of two families.

Whoever said it was easier to raise two kids than one obviously never
tried to raise six.

Let's just say the effort made my sales job seem easy.

In truth, it was all that my wife and I could do to hold the families and
our marriage together.

Wife handled the strain better than I.

She did a lot of things better than I, and one of those was falling
asleep.

She could conk out in the middle of a sentence.

Most amazing was that the sentence could be in the middle of a
heated discussion.

I would lay there impatiently waiting for her to finish a thought, when
there would be a moment of silence, followed by the telltale
sounds of slumber.

That's the way it was this particular evening: stress, strain, and
disagreement during the day, discussion in the evening, and
then sleep for my wife.

I just lay there trying to convince myself that this second marriage to a
wonderful gal with four great kids was the right move for both
of us and that together we could make it all work.

What happened next would effect me the rest of my life.

Only later, many years later, did I realize how much.

My eyes had been focused on a decorative beam that ran across the
ceiling.

Suddenly, and for what reason I cannot tell you, that same beam and
the whole room stated to shake.

I stared in disbelief, and then I started to tremble.

A wonderful calm soon followed, capturing both mind and body.

And then a feeling of joy enveloped me, and tears of happiness filled
and flooded my eyes.

It All Matters

Oh God, it was a wonderful feeling!
Joy and peace and magic all combined to create a feeling I had never
  experienced before.
And, yes, together wife and I would make our marriage work, and we
  would be a family.
Those were my thoughts as sleep carried me off.

I never told anyone;
  who would have believed such a story.
You had to be there.

THE LADY IN GREEN

My mother had recently passed away.

Mental and physical deterioration had left little of this once proud and vital woman.

The last time I saw Mom she was in the hospital, unaware of where she was and that I was with her.

I held her hand and watched her struggle for every breath.

I should have realized she was dying and stayed with her, but I didn't, and regrettably returned home, never to see her again.

Several weeks later, Elaine and I had overnight guests; our daughter and grandchild.

We were all watching TV at one end of the house.

Nature's call sent me scurrying off to the bathroom at the other end of the house.

The bathroom was adjacent to the master bedroom.

Not wanting to miss the end of the show, I turned the TV on in the master bedroom and angled a mirror on the bathroom window ledge so as to allow further viewing.

What happened next has never been logically explained, and that was some 20 years ago.

While answering mother nature's call, and at the same time intensively watching the end of the show, a figure dressed in green suddenly passed in front of the TV.

I recall yelling out, "Hey, I can't see; you're blocking my view."

The figure moved on and disappeared.

When I returned to the TV room and my wife and daughter, I asked who had been in my bedroom and why?

Both swore then and to this day, some 30 years later, that neither had left the TV room while I was away.

Neither wife nor daughter was wearing anything in green.

I have had no history of hallucinations and wasn't drinking at the time.

Furthermore, to my knowledge and theirs, no one else was in the house.

It All Matters

Yet someone, or something, dressed in green passed across my line of
      vision.

Perhaps Mom came to say goodbye, a goodbye never made at the
      hospital.
And Mom did own and frequently did wear a green sweater.
Oh, I agree, there must be a more logical explanation.
I just haven't been able to determine it.
One thing is certain, I will never again watch TV through a mirror.
I'd rather miss the program, even change my pants.

THE PAMPHLET

It was during one of those frequent stressful periods a long time ago.
Work had been more demanding than usual, and the need to increase
    income was great.
A large growing family will create that need.
It will also generate its own share of stress.
And so before long, I found falling asleep at night a major challenge.
I tried exercising before dinner, after dinner, and before retiring.
    The latter would include attacking the basement stairs and
    circling the basement floor.
It didn't work; the exercise just exaggerated the next day's fatigue, and
    I continued to wrestle with issues I considered unresolved.
Growing desperate, I turned to various sleep inducing, over the
    counter drugs.
They proved as successful as exercise.

The pamphlet came in the mail.
I had glanced at it and added it to the discard pile.
Probably because I recalled the author's name and heard of a few of
    his works, I picked up the pamphlet again and scanned
    through its pages.
The message was clear: it spoke of God, that His blessing awaited
    those who prayed for it, and that the remedy for stress and its
    related problems was a faith in Him and a trust in His
    decisions.
Now scanning became reading, and I could feel hope rising.
Was it possible that here at last was the help I sought?
I became a supporter and shortly thereafter ordered the book I had
    heard of, his book, *The Power of Positive Thinking*, by
    Norman Vincent Peale.
Beyond all expectations, his work served as the tonic I needed and
    sought. I would read from it every evening after retiring, and
    every evening my interest would grow, and after giving the
    day's problems my best effort, I would put it in His hands.
I would literally try to visualize the transfer of problems from my
    hands to His, and in so doing, I would find peace and fall
    asleep.

Such a simple approach to life's problems:
>   make the effort, do your best in every way, and then
>   "Put it in His hands" *
>   "For if God be for us, who can be against us?"
Over the years, I would reread the book many times, and it
>   would always serve me well.

There were many such messages.
I would frequently call on one in particular; whenever a challenge
>   would seem overwhelming.
Such was the case when called on to address a group of business
>   associates.
Far from a public speaker, and always fearful of failure, I needed
>   something to lean on, something to bolster my
>   self-confidence.
I found that something again in Peale's work.
As I approached the podium I silently repeated the words,
>   "I can do all things through Christ which strengthens me."**
Another tonic, for sure.
Some might even refer to it, along with a belief in God, as a "crutch,"
>   a weakness that should not be necessary, that is not
>   necessary for the strong, intelligent, and self-sufficient.

To this I say, if faith is a crutch, then consider its purpose, for if
>   faith serves to assist and overcome weakness and uncertainty,
>   and if faith inspires love and trust, then it is God's will and a
>   blessing to be welcomed and cherished.
I pray my faith will ever grow.

---

* The Power of Positive Thinking Pg 60 item 8, Pg 14 item 5
** *ibid* Pg 14, item 7

MENSCH ---- ALL

PAUL & SID

I had heard the word before.

I don't know exactly where or when or how many times, and I could
only guess its meaning.

It was a compliment of sorts, or so I believed.

Whether "Mensch" was a noun or adjective, or if it even had a plural,
I didn't know.

It's usage increased drastically when I was transferred from Ohio to
New York.

Hearing the word, "Mensch" as in, "He's a real Mensch," was as
popular as, "How ya doin'?"

And although I still didn't know, and was too embarrassed to ask its
true meaning, I kind of went along with the feeling that it
referred to a good person.

This conclusion was assumed as the individual in question always
appeared to me as just that, a good person.

But it took my new wholesale distributor and its two principals to
finally and fully explain the meaning of the word Mensch.

They being Paul and Sid.

Their exact titles were unimportant as they worked together and
shared responsibilities as good partners should.

In 20 years, I never heard an argument between them, discussions
of course, but anything controversial would be resolved in
private.

And as hard and as many times as I listened for a raised voice, I never
heard one, not once.

I remember them this way:

Paul was the outside man.

Both intelligent and well spoken, he represented his company at all
important functions, handled key accounts, and managed the
sales force.

He was never at a loss for the right words, regardless of the situation.

By all standards, Paul was a gentleman, a class act.

76

It All Matters

For me, a near rookie with his first major assignment, he was a
        tolerant, understanding, and patient man.
Once when going through a difficult divorce, I foolishly let out my
        frustrations on a customer who rightfully complained to Paul.
        Paul apologized to the customer, explaining my situation, and
        then encouraged me to personally apologize to the customer,
        which I did.
Paul's tact and understanding both saved the account and contributed
        greatly to my personal growth.
He was always there for me, as he was for his own people, always
        supportive, always kind, always the gentleman.

Sid was cut from a different cloth.
He was the office and warehouse manager, the buyer, the control guy.
He was also a no frills guy and as down-to-earth as the soil itself.
He smoked cigars when you could still do it in an office, and no one
        complained.
No words or actions were wasted and the warehouse and its inventory
        were skillfully handled, a responsibility as important as any in
        the successful operation of a distributorship.
When Sid spoke, you listened and learned.
He knew the business and made sure you did, too.
He could be curt and lacked in presentation skills, but Sid was one
        smart guy who knew and protected his business.
As I said, when Sid spoke, you listened.
And this "tough" guy had another side to him; he could also be
        thoughtful and caring.
Once, when I found reason to overreact to criticism and sought
        refuge in the warehouse, it was Sid who found me and, in his
        own "tough" way, told me to forget it and go back to work,
        which I did. As I said, you always listened to Sid.

Having lunch with them was always a special treat for me.
Joining them represented the first time I went to lunch in a Caddy.
They would put me in the back with the bowling balls.
At first it was the trunk, but then they got to trust me.
Paul would tell me not to smoke, and Sid would tell me to hold
        my breath.

It was a fifteen-minute drive to the kosher deli. I usually wasn't too
hungry by the time we got there.

They always ordered the same thing, salami and eggs.

Once, Paul ordered tuna salad on rye, and it almost ended
       their partnership.

After lunch, it was back to the Caddy and the bowling balls, and
       we were off to a grand tour of the local banks.

If one branch was crowded, they simply went to another; didn't
       matter, they had an account in almost everyone.

While they were in the bank, I remained in the Caddy guarding the
       bowling balls.

It was like I had found my niche in life, a bowling ball guard.

Listen, it wasn't easy; it took me ten years to gain their confidence.

Individually, in their own different ways, Paul and Sid taught me the
       meaning of the word Mensch: a good person, a person of
       quality with feelings for others, with respect for all, a doer,
       a contributor, in short, a person of character.

Such were Paul and Sid.

I checked Webster's New College Dictionary for the word Mensch.

It wasn't there.

It should be.

MENSCH ---- ALL

PLUMBER & SON

In the 33 years I was out in the field selling, I never met
      anyone like Frank, not anyone, not even close.
I don't know what was more unique, his physical appearance,
      or his approach to business.
Short in stature, unaccustomed to a hairbrush, and indifferent
      to both dress and speech, this former plumber was indeed
      an unlikely innovator of the retail building materials industry.
To say his approach to business was unique would be an
      understatement – revolutionary providing a far more
      appropriate description.
You have to understand that what Frank did, what he accomplished,
      was contrary to the norms of business at the time. While
      industry concentrated on inventory control, sales training, and
      advertising, Frank concentrated on depth of inventory or, if
      you will, "inventory dominance" in a limited number of lines.
While others attempted to cover all the product lines with necessarily
      limited inventory, Frank took on but a few of the more
      popular lines and dominated them.
He dominated with both quantity and variety.
If it was new and compatible with one of his lines and showed
      promise, he wanted it, and he wanted it "big."
He didn't just dip his toe in the water, he dove in.
And so, while others hesitated and pondered, Frank ordered
      and controlled.
This approach, more than anything, was the reason for his success.
I mean, where would a contractor go, where would a homeowner go,
      if variety and inventory and price were most important?
I mean, where would you go?

As a sales rep for a national manufacturer, it took me awhile to realize
      how correct this little, unassuming guy was in his approach.

Understand that my background, and therefore my sales approach,
    focused on what I had been taught and what was popular at
    the time – inventory turnover, sales training, and advertising.
For years, I would try to sell Frank on the importance of these basics
    of business, and for years Frank would ask me to check his
    inventory and place an order.
The matter was finally and forever decided when my home office,
    unable to believe my stories and Frank's success, sent
    someone special out to investigate.
If that was a mistake, the second one was worse: questioning Frank on
    those same issues of turnover, training, and advertising,
I wrote Frank's replies down:
    "Who needs turnover?
        – Turnover means more handling."
    "Don't train my people.
        – They'll know more than I will."
    "Can't advertise.
        – Won't be able to handle the business."
He concluded with,
    "Miami today, Jerusalem tomorrow."

The special home office guy didn't or couldn't respond.
He left the company shortly thereafter for a totally different
    line of work. True story.
I did what I had to. I accepted Frank's philosophy. I mean, how do
    you argue with success?
And in time, I would write my own orders, with Frank's major
    concern being that I would not order enough.
If you haven't figured it out yet, Frank was a Mensch, my Mensch.
I loved the guy and will both remember and be grateful to him for as
    long as I have a memory.
He taught me that innovation didn't necessarily start with the
    manufacturer.
He guaranteed my success as a salesman and made sure that at least
    one day of the week was enjoyable.

Most appreciated was the trust he placed in me and the free reign to order when and what I saw appropriate.

It wasn't long before this former plumber, using ideas my company
        didn't understand, presided over one of the top outlets for my
        product lines and others in the country.

When Frank retired, his son Robbie took over.
Rob practiced most all of his father's techniques and introduced
        a few of his own.
Most noteworthy, he brought his father's business into the
        21st century, adding the latest in computer technology
        and yes, believe it or not, TV advertising.
And Robbie added something else, something his father never would
        have thought of, he added a piano and the ability to play it.
Many of my sales calls there, regardless of their importance, would
        necessarily begin with Robbie at the piano requesting the name
        of any tune from the turn of the century, and I'm referring to
        the 20th century. If you couldn't come up with one, which was
        usually the case with me, he'd play several of his own
        choosing.
        Let me tell you, it was an experience.
Robbie was also a caring and generous person. Lunch was always
        on him, and he always had something to give you, some token
        or other, enough to make you feel your efforts were
        appreciated.

And then there was the time back spasms put me down and out.
        The first day home there was a knock on our front door,
        and there was Robbie with an electrical impulse gadget of
        sort, something new that he thought might help.
If you're thinking another Mensch, you got it right.

I worked with Robbie for a decade or so, and knew that their business
        would continue to grow under his guidance.
I'm retired now and for thirteen years have lived in another state,
        and Robbie still occasionally calls to say hello.
And whenever in his area, I make it a point, to stop in for a chat.
Invariably the chat leads to lunch and then a piano rendition of a turn
        of the century classic.

I spoke to Frank recently and could tell he was proud of
      his son's accomplishments.
"Like father , like son," I said.
Frank replied, "Yes, but No; Robbie works."
I don't miss much about my thirty-plus years of selling, but I do miss
      Frank and Robbie and the special relationship we shared.
Good people, lots of character.
Mensch — both.

MY LITTLE BLACK BOOK

It was always with me.

It fit snuggly into the breast pocket of my button down shirt.

It represented both my security and my advantage.

It was my little black book.

I had been working for a major building supply manufacturer as a sales representative for a number of years.

Important notes were at first kept anywhere and everywhere, or sometimes not at all.

Then they were collected in a notebook and finally condensed and placed in a little black book.

It was all there, most everything I needed to support a sales call:

- names and functions of all key personnel
- phone numbers of all accounts
- technical data too complicated to remember
- general data I had trouble remembering
- specific goals and the means to accomplish those goals for each of my top 50 accounts
- selling techniques for different product lines
- directions for out-of-my-way or difficult-to-find accounts
- weekly travel schedules
- weekly expenses

A tug at my shirt pocket, a flip of the cover, a turn of a page, and I had the information I needed.

It proved easy and effective, and it wasn't long before my reputation grew as being well organized.

Over a period of 33 years, I had four regional managers.

All applauded the little black book and encouraged others to develop a similar approach.

To keep the contents current it would be updated and rewritten at the beginning of each year.

Life was good.

My career was good, and my efforts and results were acknowledged and rewarded.

I was on a roll and, at least in my eyes, I was a success.

I climbed the ladder of titles and was given greater responsibility.

As I said, I was on a roll, and my little black book had a great deal to
do with it – always there, always guiding, always providing.

But alas, there is little that is more precarious than success, and too
often the first declining step goes unnoticed.

So it was in my 30th year of selling, when a new progressive national
sales manager equipped the entire sales force with what at the
time was the latest technology in communication,
the cell phone.

Although I had some trouble familiarizing myself with it, as anything
new and different created a prolonged period of adjustment
for me, I soon realized that the cell phone had its advantages.

Most importantly, I no longer had to stop to make a phone call, and
so it wasn't long before a few pages of cell phone numbers
were added to my little black book.

Once again, everything was in order, under control, yet I could not
help but notice the tug at my security.

And as it turned out, the listing of cell phone numbers represented the
last major entry into my black book, as shortly thereafter
the computer exploded on the scene, marking the beginning of
the end of my career and my little black book.

I had heard the rumor that the computer was on its way, and had, with
my wife's patient assistance and her computer, struggled
through an introductory course.

So I wasn't entirely computer ignorant when the "demon" arrived, just
mostly.

An all-day orientation class was immediately scheduled and run by my
company.

I, and other elders, had trouble keeping up with the class, while the
juniors were right there often working ahead of the instructor.

It was not a good feeling.

I was too old to be a freshman.

The "down" feeling grew worse when a few rookies, who were not
old enough to be my son, offered assistance.

I didn't know whether to thank them or send them to their rooms.

As I said, it was not a good feeling. The training class at last over, I
headed home.

It All Matters

But there was no escape, for there waiting for me was my very own
computer wrapped in enough cardboard to protect a
breakfront.

With wife's help, we freed the "demon," and there, with me watching,
wife hooked it up.

According to her, I was in business.

I wasn't so sure.

The first few months really weren't so bad. Usage was limited to
weekly expense reports and an occasional "how you doin'?"
message from the field.

What once took fifteen minutes to complete by hand, now
took me forty-five minutes with the computer.

Whoever said, "If it ain't broke, don't fix it" should have spoken
louder, slower, and more frequently.

Most troublesome was answering the messages, as my typing skills
were limited to whatever output my right hand index finger
could provide.

I was painfully slow, and when at last a return message was completed,
it would invariably fail to include something important.

And so, rather than go through the laborious process again,
I would call, a regular, old-fashioned telephone call, and
discuss in detail whatever needed to be discussed.

It wasn't long before I would just bypass the computer entirely and
place a phone call, allowing for a free, complete, and
instantaneous exchange of ideas.

This breach of procedure didn't last long, however, as the number of
incoming messages ever increased with more and more
messages coming from management and requiring a computer
reply.

I had no choice, and each night would get later as I pecked away with
my one productive finger.

More and more time was spent receiving and sending messages.

As a result, sales calls became fewer and fewer and planned sales calls
made the endangered list.

I think this bothered me most because what I enjoyed most about my
job was selling – a product, a promotion, an idea.

First came the idea, then the plan, then the presentation.

Success came with some, failure with others, but failure only made the successes all the sweeter.

The computer ended this, my approach to selling, for it became the "grinch" that stole selling time, too often its contribution incomplete and/or inappropriate.

As a senior sales representative, one of my responsibilities was to travel with and assist the new and inexperienced, the rookie.

This would include making sales calls with them, critiquing their efforts, and offering suggestions.

The computer changed all this, and what was once a rewarding experience for me now became a waste of time and an embarrassment.

The "new" were now looking for that which I could not provide: computer advice, computer techniques, computer, computer, computer.

It was like they were under a spell, like the selling process began and ended with the computer, like one couldn't sell without a computer, like developing selling skills and making sales calls were secondary, and "Hey, by the way, what's that little black book in your pocket?"

And then they, the "new," would demonstrate their computer skills, and I unable to contribute, could do no more than nod in agreement.

As I said, it was all very embarrassing, and before long the computer message became clear-time and technology had passed me by.

Most everything comes to an eventual end, and so it was with me and my little black book.

It was now rarely referred to and even more rarely recommended.

The computer age had arrived, changing business as I had known it.

As for me, the necessary adjustment was too severe, the leap too great.

But what the hell, I had had my run and enjoyed my successes.

It was time for someone else's "little black book."

I never did discard mine, the last one, I mean.

Once in a while I come across it in my file cabinet, flip the cover, turn the page, and remember how good it was, how good it all was, once upon a time.

FOOLISH OR FOOLED

It's been more than ten years since I left my life's work, and I still
haven't been able to determine whether I just made a dumb
move or was taken advantage of by those I trusted.

Allow me to relate to you the circumstances as I recall them, as
impartially as I can, and then ask you to decide: was I foolish
or was I fooled?

I was employed for some 33 years at various levels of selling
and marketing for a major manufacturer of "whatever."

The product itself has no bearing on the story, and, as things turned
out, the corporation was like most any other, so that
information shall also be omitted.

Know that I worked hard. There was no clock to punch, and most
weekdays would find me at my desk working until 8:00 or 9:00
in the evening, and it was rare that a weekend was free of
work. Little or no time went for hobbies. What free time I had
went to my family and to the upkeep of my house.

If you call that dedication, you'd be half right, the other half
being fear of failure. Even worse, when after years of service
and vacation time had doubled, I would waive several weeks
each year because the job and succeeding came first.

And succeed I did:

- The only years I did not meet or exceed budget was the years of
  either economic depression or factory shut downs, and those years
  were few and far between.

- In the 33 years of service there were fewer than a handful when
  my salary was not adjusted upward. Not once did I find it
  necessary to request additional salary compensation. It was always
  there for me, and over the years it would increase enough to
  provide for a comfortable living.

- Acknowledgement also came in a variety of other ways: trophies
  and plaques and mugs and desk accessories, dinners and get away
  weekends with spouse, tickets to ball games, Super Bowl
  weekends, and numerous letters and articles of commendation
  from all levels of management, many of which would come at the
  time of my retirement. I was nominated twice and winner once of

the much coveted divisional salesman-of-the year award, which brought with it numerous shares of company stock and a substantial salary increase. It is fact that in the 33 years that I was there, no one ever won the award twice, and very few were nominated twice.

- For many years, I was responsible for one of the largest divisional sales territory in the United States.
- Numerous job title changes brought with it additional responsibilities including traveling with and counseling new representatives and serving on various national sales advisory committees.
- As time passed and the market changed, I would become responsible for the larger and more productive accounts.

There is more, but perhaps that's enough to convince you that I was appreciated and acknowledged by many as the # 1 sales representative in the division. The "ultimate professional" were the words I heard most often. And yes, I both welcomed and appreciated them.

There is of course the other side of the coin. There always is. With reference to that side, I will relate all that I know as fact, and some of what I believe:

- In the beginning, in the '60s, business was widespread, coming from a great variety of both large and small accounts. Market coverage, therefore, was seen to require an extended sales force provided by both manufacturer and wholesaler.
- The change in the market would be ever so gradual. It would also be definite and undeniable, as more and more business would come from fewer and fewer accounts. This rate of change would accelerate through the '70s and '80s. As a result, the smaller independents would become less and less of a factor and, therefore, require less and less attention.
- The responsibility for calling on these smaller accounts would fall to the wholesaler salesman, thus allowing the manufacturer's representative to concentrate on the larger, more productive accounts.

- The greatest change in the market would come with the advent of the superstore: the giant chain stores, the Home Depots, Lowes, and others.
They would appear throughout the country and before long dominate most every product line they took on, including ours.
- Local chains and highly specialized independents would also grow in importance and take a good share of the market.
- And so the market would change with fewer and fewer accounts taking more and more business. This concentration of business would lessen the need for the rep as he was and give rise to the large account rep whose focus would be on the "high rollers," the big boys, the controllers of an increasing percentage of the market. Towards the end of my career, I became one such large-account representative.
- This latest change would serve to expand my territory geographically while reducing my account number. For me, it would also be my last change, unless you wish to include retirement.

I must have seen myself as irreplaceable with a long record of
achievements and a large number of well established contacts
and relationships.
How could my company possibly do without me?
Surely, if the time had come for personnel reductions, it wouldn't
affect me, not this decorated specialist with 33 years
of impeccable, undeniably productive, and loyal service.
Someone else perhaps, but not the division's #1 sales representative,
not the "ultimate professional," not in a million years!
No, "not in a million years," – just now!

Allow me to set the stage for the "Great Divide,"
again, as I recall it, as fairly as I can.
It was at a sales meeting at the close of my thirty-third year of service.
The national sales manager pulled me aside and informed me of yet
additional changes to be made in sales territory and
responsibility.
He described what was coming as a new period of attrition, and then
he inquired whether I wanted to try to hang on or should he

look into a retirement package for me. I received his words as
a warning from a friend, since I previously had worked for and
with him.
And then I agreed to the alternative, the "look see."

It didn't take long, perhaps a week or so, when another meeting was
called between the same national manager, the area manager,
and yours truly, the guy they were in charge of.
What was presented was a new recently improved retirement package
of which I was entirely unaware.
The new package was presented entirely by the "main" man.
And present he did, comparing the old and new in great detail, with
emphasis on the added improvements.
I perceived it at that time and to this day as a selling effort with the
intended purpose of gaining my retirement.

My intention was to retire at 62, but the improved package,
combined with a future that was described as uncertain,
together with what I considered the company's true intention,
made retirement the logical move at age 57.
I have to say, I was not pressured to accept, but rather encouraged
to think it over.
When I left to drive home, I think I already knew that I would accept,
that the curtain was falling on my career.
In my opinion, they knew it too. They knew my best was behind me,
that I was tired and prone to accepting an offer. Again, my
opinion.
The drive home was long and difficult.
As I recall, I cried enough to redden my eyes.
I was losing a major portion of my life and finding the reality
of it overwhelming.

At home and after a long discussion with my wife, we agreed it
was time to "cut the cord."
The next morning, I called my area manager who had said nothing,
not a word, at the new retirement package presentation.
This was my immediate boss, someone I had worked with for years,
and I believed shared a good relationship with.
His opinion was important to me, and so I called.

It All Matters

He voiced none. Speaking calmly and deliberately, he made it quite
        clear that the decision was mine to make, mine alone.

There was no advice or opinion given.

Although surprised and disappointed at what I took as indifference,
        wife and I stayed with the decision to accept the retirement
        offer.

Play over. Curtain down.

In the weeks and months to follow we would put our house up for
        sale and plan a relocation in the south.

To supplement my income, I would gain temporary employment with
        a local distributor and continue selling my former company's
        product line, along with a few others.

It was nice: less work, less pressure, and my total income was
        comparable to before retirement.

That "good" feeling would come to an abrupt end with a phone call
        from a former associate and lasting friend who had just
        accepted the now "latest" retirement offer.

He had previously been upset because he had just missed qualifying
        for the offer extended to and accepted by me.

Now he was ecstatic with this latest offer:
        a multi-thousand dollar settlement spread out over several
        years to minimize taxes, plus a gift of additional years of
        service to substantially increase his monthly pension.

This all-new, latest offer came months after mine.

If my friend was ecstatic, I was a combination of despondent,
        devastated, and dumbfounded.

I wasn't big enough to be happy for him, I was hurting too much.

Our years of service, our sales records and accomplishments were
        comparable, and I'm being more than fair, as I believe my sales
        were generally greater.

And yet, despite these similarities of record, there was this vast and
        unexplainable difference in the retirement packages offered
        within months of each other.

At first I couldn't believe it.

Then I couldn't understand it.

How could this happen? Why?

When I gained enough composure to speak, I asked just that. How?
        Why?

Apparently my former associate and still friend was a lot smarter
than I. He played a game that I didn't know existed.

For lack of better wordage, let's call it "the retirement game."

Realizing the company was in the process of downsizing, he clearly
voiced his intention to work until seventy, the maximum age
one could work at the time.

A few failed negotiations later, he was offered the package he
accepted, the new grandiose offer previously described, the
offer far superior to mine.

And yes, the offer was presented by the same national sales manager
who had presented mine, and who upon being asked by me,
before any papers had been signed, if any additional changes in
the retirement packages were forthcoming, had emphatically
replied, "NO."

I felt like such a damn fool.

For 33 years I had put all my faith in my company and its
people, and for 33 years this approach had worked
fairly and justly for me – always taken care of, always
acknowledged, always rewarded.

Why should retirement change anything?

It did, and I was "dead" wrong in my assumptions.

Retirement had become a process of negotiation, a game of strategy,
and yes, a game of hardball.

I felt betrayed, deceived, taken advantage of.

And as I said, I felt like such a damn fool.

Well, there you have it, as much as I can recall and as fairly as I can
present it.

You be the judge.

Was I just naïve and made a foolish error in judgment, or was I treated
unfairly, tricked, taken advantage of?

I can accept either judgment and personally lean towards a
combination of the two.

More importantly, however, was the effect the experience had on me
and the hard lessons I hopefully learned.

With emphasis on the latter they are:

It All Matters

- Business is business,
    first, last, and always.
- No one is irreplaceable,
    no one.
- Trust always with caution,
    and never 100 percent.
- We are molded by events and people:
    all that occurs in one's lifetime,
    all people, all experiences, all joys and sorrows,
    all accomplishments and failures, all struggles,
    they all, to some extent, affect.
    They all matter.

So what's next?
I know there's more to come and more to learn.
I can only hope that now I am better prepared, more aware, less naïve,
    and if you will, a shark on the hunt.
And if you won't buy that, how about a minnow on the move?

DEFINING SUCCESS
Letter to alumni magazine

I was just wondering if anyone in the Class of '56, or for that matter, any other class, has led as undistinguished, mundane, and uneventful life as I have?

I was never an executive, director, president, board member, consultant, or strategic planner.

I never traveled the world or started a business.

I never took a postgraduate course, painted a picture, or became computer proficient.

Rather, my life went something like this:

After graduating from Rutgers University, I worked in NYC as a building products sales representative where I spent more time commuting from New Jersey than I did working in New York. Six months later I found myself in the US Army at Fort Bliss, TX, where I spent most of the next two years making a baby, hiding from the sun, and wondering why I took ROTC. The next 33 years were even more exciting. I sired another baby and then found a quicker way to grow a family: I married a gal with four kids. If you're counting, that makes a grand total of six. And, believe me, that's exciting.

Career-wise, the same 33 years were spent with yet another building supply manufacturer where I served once again as a sales representative.

But I was good. So good in fact, that I was eventually awarded the title of Senior Building Product Sales Representative, which meant I was getting old.

And eventually, if you can believe it, Territory Manager, which meant I was now credited with managing my territory as opposed to just running it.

How I avoided a swollen head, I'll never know.

Now I'm retired, living off Social Security and his and her pension checks.

I sleep late, exercise seldom, imbibe in abundance, and watch my girth grow.

How's that for a success story?

PART III

SUNSHINE

Sunshine's my name
     and casting shadow's my game.

I'm also known as Easy Al
     and status quo's my pal.

A MARRIAGE TOAST

When I first met Barbara, my wife's niece, she was crawling around in
her crib.
Not that that was unusual; she was a baby.
What I found unusual was that her parents, Howie and Alice, were
crawling around in the same crib with her.
You might say they loved, cherished, and adored Barbara.
You might also be understating their feelings.

And the love never faltered, never, ever.
When Barbara outgrew her crib and started crawling around the
house, her parents followed right along. Not that that was
unusual; she was a baby.
What I found unusual was that they crawled along beside her.
Throughout her public school years they were always there for her
and frequently with her.
I doubt that a child ever received more love, care, and attention.
Put it this way, nothing, no event, no person came before Barbara,
and she wore her tiara well.
When Barbara went south for her college education, Howie and Alice
took to their car and found a new way to spend weekends.
When Barbara met Mitch, he was welcomed with open arms into their
love nest. Mitch became "Mitchie" and Barbara "Barbie."
I had heard a lot about Mitch and finally got to meet him at a party
at Barbara's house in New Jersey.
I remember that I couldn't understand him.
Then Barbara came along, and I couldn't understand her either.
It was embarrassing; we all stood there smiling and nodding our
heads, and no one knew what the other was saying.
I had never heard anything like it before. Barbara had a drawl, so you
had some time between vowels to translate.
Mitich on the other hand, used a rapid fire assault, with half
of every word missing.
I'd be working on the first few words, and he'd be waiting for a reply.
It was Howie and Alice who came over to serve as interpreters.
With their help, I learned that Mitch had previously spent some time

in the Bronx.

I asked him, "In what country?"

He replied "Alabama."

Howie, Alice, and Barbara all nodded in agreement.

Not important. Tomorrow is important.

Tomorrow is their big day. Barbara and Mitch are getting married.

I have to tell you, I'm a little concerned. I have to wonder if
Howie and Alice will be joining them on their honeymoon?

And of even more concern, what will happen when, during the
ceremony, the big moment finally arrives and Mitch is
asked, "Will you?" And he answers, "Ah will, y'all."

Understand, this minister is from New Jersey. He's likely to
baptize Mitch.

Oh, what am I worried about? They have love.

These two have love from all sides, from everyone.

It's almost sickening.

But most important of all, they understand each other, and the fact
that no one else does, doesn't matter.

I wish them, in addition to love, understanding, patience, and
forgiveness
(and a speech therapist wouldn't hurt either).

EPILOGUE

Barbara and Mitch currently reside in Birmingham, Alabama, where
they lovingly raise two sons with, of course, the ongoing
love, care, and attention of Howie and Alice.

I am unable to understand either child.

"CHECKBOOK" JANET

Some 27 years after our wedding dinner, the same happy
     foursome was traveling in the southeast in search of a utopian
     place to retire.
The last stop of the last day brought us to a place in the lowlands
     with few trees, fewer homes, and unpaved roads.
The sales office was in a trailer neatly nestled in a mud bank. Everyone
     wanted to leave except Janet, so we stayed.
You could tell Janet was interested because she stopped yelling
     at Alan.
Realizing our vulnerability, the developer made his move, successfully
     dividing us into two groups. The first group, Elaine and I,
     politely sat and listened and being generally unimpressed,
     began to leave.
It was on our way out that all our lives changed.
There, in a room similar to the one we had just left, was the second
     group, Janet and Alan. Janet was smiling and writing
     something in her checkbook. Alan was either expiring or in
     the process thereof. There was no color in his face. Lifeless
     eyes stared straight ahead. His face was sullen and he appeared
     infinitely frightened.
He could only softly moan as Janet triumphantly closed her
     checkbook. "I have a good feeling about this place,"
     she explained, as Elaine and I attempted to revive Alan.

Alan fully recovered and was to become "Billy Bob" of Calabash.
Elaine and Al were to catch the same "good feeling" and buy in the
     same retirement community.
And so it goes with the best yet to come, or so we thought.

It All Matters
NOW IS HERE

I remember the brochure described the weather as "temperate,"
      meaning mild, gentle, calm, easy. (I looked it up.)
It sounded wonderful to my wife and me, and the thought of
      spending our retirement years in a plantation community with
      its own golf course, pool, restaurant, and recreational center
      was more than we could ignore. In short, we retired, waved
      Auf Wiedersehen to our family and moved from
      snowy, chilly New York to sunny, warm North Carolina.

We are here ten years now. In that time we have experienced
      five hurricanes, two northeasters, four draughts, the hottest
      summer and coldest winters on record, more tropical storms
      than Tahiti, a much too close tornado, and the
      "Flood of the Century."
If that's moderate, then I'm the Jolly Green Giant.
I mean, I'm not much for snow and ice, but what's so great about
      changing your undies three times a day?
I didn't find "sticky" anywhere in Webster's definition of moderate.
And then there are the daily thunderstorms.
I haven't crawled under a bed so much since I was a boy.
Mom used to explain that a thunderstorm was really God bowling
      in heaven. What Mom didn't tell me was that God's favorite
      lanes were in North Carolina.
Wife was never one to miss an opportunity, so whenever the sky
      would light up and the thunder reign down, wife would
      invariably hand me a seven iron and tell me to go out and
      practice my chipping.
After awhile, I caught on and replaced the iron with a wood.
Intelligence is such a blessing.

The spring here brings daily showers. I mean daily! I mean every day!
The natives all say the same thing, "When April showers come your
      way, they bring the flowers that bloom in May."
The transplants respond with, "When April showers come your way,
      you know damn well there's more in May."
A solution to the rain came unexpectedly.

I was lying in bed, staring at the ceiling, which is usually what I do in
bed now, when a voice came from above and it said to me,
"Derfla (that's what my friends call me) build an ark and
collect two of each."

You don't argue with something like that.

So I built an ark and started collecting.

The insects weren't a problem; I found most every kind in my
living room.

Animals, however, were a problem. I couldn't find any.

And then it dawned on me, the insects ate them.

That's why they're so damn big.

Soon my neighbors caught my drift, and they too started building
and collecting.

And before long we became a community of many arks and fewer
insects.

The plantation also introduced me to what the natives refer to as
"no-see-ums." No one can tell you what they look like because
no one can see them. You just feel the hell out of them and
scratch yourself until you realize you're bleeding. That's when
you know you have a "no-see-um" problem.

I'm not going to get into mosquitoes as they exist most everywhere.

Just know that here they are four times as large and four times as
many, and should it be your misfortune to be bitten twice in
the same day, life demands a blood transfusion.

But my favorite plantation "pet" is that playful, adorable, little
Japanese beetle that spends half its time eating and the other
half copulating. I really should have been a beetle.

I mean, eating's great, but my body calls for more.

Once I took wife out to observe the beetles in action, figuring it might
help our situation.

She said she didn't understand.

Then she brought me inside, threw a brown coat over my shoulders,
and sprayed me with Sevin solution. She understood!

Not my favorite, but definitely a force to be reckoned with are the
local frogs that "bark," and leave their "calling cards"
anywhere they please, but usually on a pane of glass or door
– not nice!

It All Matters

Even more charming is their reaction to the human touch. There is no
 way you can pick one up in an effort to remove it without
 being "whizzed" on.
I could have said urinated, but these frogs don't urinate, they "whiz,"
 and I hate them dearly.
Another local insect is so ugly one just avoids it.
Never mind trying to kill it. That would mean getting close to it.
So you walk away and hope it will settle elsewhere.
And they just appear, like overnight.
You wake one morning and there are the "uglies," on your lawn
 staring at you, and I swear they're saying, "Yankee Go Home."

A few words regarding the soil here.
Know that it's little more than clay.
Turn a spadeful over, and with the sun's help and a limited amount of
 time, your spadeful of clay will turn to an indestructible mass
 of cement.
This might readily explain the relatively low cost of property and taxes
 in this area.
It might also explain why nothing green, other than a limited number
 of native bushes and trees, and a wonderful variety of weeds,
 survive.
You plant your naive selection in the spring, and replace it in the fall.
And in the mean time, you either spend a hundred dollars a month for
 water, or in the more likely case of flooding a hundred dollars
 for mops and hip boots.

There is one little creature, however, that thrives in this soil.
It doesn't take one long to find one of their mounds, and it takes
 even less time to realize these little "demons" defend and
 protect their privacy with their lives.
I'm talking fire ants, and I'm talking mean, fearless, antisocial devils
 that will attack anything that disturbs them.
And know that their bite is for real and that their bite infects.
Numerous bites may require medical attention.
Once when playing golf, I laid a club down on what I thought was just
 grass. It was also a mound of "devils."
Unknowingly, I picked the club up and continued my game.
After three holes of scratching, I asked a friend to see if he could

determine the reason for my discomfort. He suggested I
remove my shirt, which I did, and there, low and behold,
were the mound's inhabitants.

That evening I counted some thirty already infected bites.

Being the rugged, outdoor type, I did not go to the doctor, but I'll tell
you vodka never tasted better than it did that evening.

Needless to say, picnics and barefoot strolls are not the community's
most popular activities.

My revenge comes from thrashing their mounds with any long branch
I can find.

This causes the earth to suddenly open up, and thousands of little red
"devils" rise and search the area for the intruder.

Dropping the branch quickly, and moving away just as quickly,
are essential for good health.

The thought of their having a keen sense of smell or a good memory
is not comforting to this intruder.

Of course we have snakes.

What self-respecting plantation doesn't?

During The "Flood of the Century" we had water moccasins cruising
the flooded streets. On occasion, I have also seen them
basking on the lake rocks immediately off the golf course. Such a
sight does wonders to speed up a game.

Unidentified others have found their way into our garage
and driveway. Still others have found refuge under our
grill cover on the patio. I assume they were searching for the
barking frogs. Had I known, I would have gladly served as
their guide.

So I guess the lesson to be learned here is obvious: know when to go
out and what to wear and, most importantly, always be armed.
Survival, that's what life here is all about.

One of the plantation community's more enjoyable events is the
Garden of the Month contest.

This is where a self-elected committee surveys the plantation area and
selects that property most closely resembling the Biltmore Estates.

Wife and I have always tried our best to win this most coveted prize.

We always made sure the lawn was mowed, bushes trimmed, beds
cleaned out, driveway swept.

It All Matters

We put "NEW" signs on all healthy bushes and pulled the others.
And once in an all out-effort, wife had me stand in the driveway with
        a gardenia in my mouth.
Nothing – not even an honorable mention.
When wife suggested I relocate the gardenia, I knew it was time to
        seek another prize. I mean, I wanted to win, but not that bad.

A few words regarding my wife:
- Can you believe it, she lives with me, and they call her an angel?
- She does her thing all day and then, when it's time for dinner, we go out, because our new kitchen is too large. At the restaurant we sit at different tables to avoid arguing.
- Sometime around 8:00 p.m. she falls asleep, and when I pick her up and carry her to bed, she whispers, "don't touch me."
- Not since the "Flood of the Century" have I heard,
        "The ceiling needs painting."

I'm kidding, of course.
My little white haired angel is everything to me.
She is my companion, my confidant, my love.
She is also my social agent and partner.
And it is because of her that we live in a new house on the 18th
        hole of a golf course, have new friends, new activities, and
        a new way of life.
The beautiful days of spring and fall, the snowless winters,
        the magnificent sunsets are all here to be enjoyed.
And when all is said and done and all things are considered,
        and I face and accept what is important and what is not,
        I come to the undeniable conclusion that, at my age,
        at this time of my life, I am where I belong.

Now don't get me wrong, New York, with all its boroughs and
        suburbs has its advantages. It is a fully loaded entertainment
        center with something for everyone.
And the weather is less extreme with far fewer hurricanes, no
        tornados, and negligible flooding.
And what's a little snow now and then, especially if your wife
        has a giving disposition and a strong back.
And the insects are normal. There are no fire ants, no no-see-ums,

no barking frogs, far fewer beetles, and smaller mosquitoes.
In some 60 years, I never saw a snake,
And there is soil that grows most everything.
There are the Yankees, Giants, Knicks, Rangers, some other
lesser teams.
There is pizza with a crust, real bread, the best restaurants of every
kind, Broadway shows, Manhattan shopping, and anything
else one might possibly want.

Now top that off with exploding land and house values, small
kitchens, and ceilings that always need painting, if you catch
my drift, and you have the best of New York.
But, alas, New York also has many millions of people and therefore
more than its share of traffic, congestion, slums, violence and
crime, trash and clutter, dirt and disease.
Not surprising, it has become a beehive of tension and anxiety. Its
inhabitants having little choice but to join what has been aptly
described as "the rat race." Dialects, accents, and slang abound
and join together to form unique, and in many cases,
unintelligible versions of the English language.
A greeting might well be "How ya doin'?"
An argument might well include, " You talkin' to me?"
In short, New York is a world in itself, spinning in an
ever-accelerating orbit.
An exciting place to live, yes, when you're young and strong and
ambitious and when making money is the all-driving force and
also the reward.
But for me, all that is "then."
For me, "now" is sleeping late, playing golf, traveling, dining out
frequently, and almost always doing what I want, when I want.
For me now is here.

PROMISE THEM ANYTHING

I was running for a relatively unimportant office in my relatively
      unimportant retirement community.
The following was posted for all to see:
      I, Al Strohmayer, accept the nomination for area
      representative.
      Some important facts for your consideration:

      I was born in Flushing, New York in 1934.
      The hospital bill was $80.
      My father said it was a rip-off.
      He and my mother were hoping for a girl, so they
          called me Nancy.
      It was not until my thirteenth birthday that I was able to
          convince my parents that a dress was inappropriate.
      I tell you this so you will better understand why
          I am the way I am.

I run on a program of principles:

1. Equal opportunity for all men
2. Removal of all Taliban from the community
3. Placement of storm troopers at the front entrance
4. In-depth commando training for all
5. A pooper scooper in every home

I realize it's a lot to promise, but I'm a man of my word,
      and I'm not a crook.

EPILOGUE

I won in a landside.
The fact that no one ran against me mattered little.
I would have beaten Bill Clinton.

LET IT SNOW

LET IT SNOW

LET IT SNOW

A stranger just walked up the slope behind my house leading
      to the ninth tee.
He walked slowly and uncertainly.
He appeared confused, even lost.
When he teed off in the wrong direction, I knew he was in trouble.
And no wonder, the barometer at 11:00 a.m. on my patio read
      100 degrees, meaning the heat index approached 110 degrees,
      meaning by the afternoon it would get even hotter.
It's that way today.
It was that way yesterday.
It will be that way tomorrow.
Since the end of June, the weather here, promoted as "temperate",
      meaning moderate according to Webster, has been swelteringly
      hot, oppressively humid, and basically breezeless.
Only a daily thunderstorm brings a breeze, and as that serves as a
      warning as to what is yet to come, one generally isn't outside
      to enjoy it.

To go outside is to sweat, and no, I don't mean perspire, for the
      word perspire is intended for humans under "normal"
      conditions.
The weather here is not "normal," and so, like an animal, you sweat.
And so, like a human, I made a commitment to stay inside and enjoy
      one of man's gifts to mankind, air conditioning.
Unfortunately, it wasn't long before enjoyment turned to boredom,
      and then depression.
I mean, even with a keen imagination such as mine, in time you
      simply run out of things to do inside.

How many times can you review your finances, upgrade your files,
     clean out your desk, and shine the family shoes?

We're talking months here, months of "animal" weather.

If you're into TV, that will help some, if you don't grow tired of
     repetitious news, car chases, documentaries about pyramids,
     survival adventures, and reality TV.

Likewise, a computer can also serve you well, if you can tolerate a stiff
     neck, an aching back, blurred vision, and an assortment of
     computer malfunctions, not all of which are virus related.

Finding nothing to hold my attention, and looking for a source of
     adventure, I turned to napping – napping in the morning,
     napping in the afternoon, napping whenever I could.

Nothing like a good dream to make you realize there's more to life
     than reality.

Unfortunately, day napping made night sleeping nearly impossible,
     and before long, I found myself relying on sleeping pills for a
     good night's rest.

I mean, I know better. A sleeping pill is a demon by any measure, yet
     staying awake all night is not a welcome alternative.

Without question, a life-style change was in order, one that would get
     me off the couch, on my feet, and out of the house.

And so I conceived a plan.

I would either play golf or work outside early each morning, before
     the worst of the day's heat could settle in.

This of course meant rising before my usual "up and at 'um"
     hour of 10:00 a.m.

And that, of course, was difficult, as by nature and habit, I was a
     "night" person, retiring late and then reading until sleep
     would come.

But I did it! I really did! I was up by 8:00 a.m. and by 9:00 I was
     outside playing the diligent homeowner.

I removed dead plants, trimmed hedges, pulled and sprayed weeds,
     and cleaned gutters.

I fertilized most everything that had a chance of growing and some
     things that didn't.

And, oh yes, I waxed two cars.

It All Matters

I did all this while flailing away at a variety of flying things
> determined to get to know me better.

And I did all this while sweating more than I ever have in my life;
> more than in any job I ever held, more than in basic training,
> and more than in two years of military service in El Paso, TX,
> where you don't need a pan to fry an egg.

When the slightest activity causes perspiration, then it's either very,
> very hot, or you're in hell.

Either way, I stuck it out for several days.

I got up early and worked outside and accomplished quite a bit.
> All things considered, I felt I had confronted the enemy
> and he was mine.

It must have been the afternoon of the second day when I first felt
> the discomfort of a sore throat.

The next day brought little change: no fever, or cough, just a
> persistent sore throat and a rapidly growing desire
> to go inside and stay there.

And that's what I did – I went inside.

Looking back, I think it must have been allergies.

I mean, if the area is conducive to breeding the insects of the world,
> then surely these same conditions are conducive to growing
> every conceivable type of spore.

Anyway, I'm back inside with my AC. Other than taking the dog
> for as brief a walk as possible (and then only when she howls),
> running an occasional errand, going out for an occasional
> dinner, or visiting a doctor, I'm in.

The outside be damned. Let the insects have it.

Maybe they'll develop an allergy.

I just wonder if hurricane conditions fall under the "temperate"
> umbrella, for we live in a hurricane alley, and this is the time of
> year for the "big breeze."

We've had them before, all kinds, and so far we've been lucky, but the
> number of storms seem to increase each year, and you wonder
> if the next one will have your name on it.

It's thundering now and raining, and the sun is out all at the
same time.

And I wonder if such a condition is common to a "temperate"
climate.

Only one thing is clear to me: another summer like this one, and I'm
out of here.

I'll go to Alaska, the North Pole, the South Pole, anywhere the
weather isn't described as temperate.

I'll build igloos, drive a sled, breed huskies, anything as long as I can
breathe easily, perspire normally, and don't play host to the
flying, crawling inhabitants of a so-called temperate climate.

AH, THE JOY OF DISCOVERY

The same question haunts my everyday.
Why do so few people talk to me?
Why are most of my conversations with myself?
And why does my dog seek shelter whenever I address her?
When the telephone rings, it's invariably for my wife.
When the doorbell rings, it's either FED EX delivering something my
       wife ordered or UPS delivering something my wife ordered.
When I go for a walk with my dog, people turn around and go the
       other way, and I know they like the dog.
When I play golf, I find myself alone in the cart.
Once I tried tennis, but got tired of fetching my own ball.
And I'm not fast enough to play ping-pong by myself.
At home, I went so far as to put a "ENTER HERE" sign in my
       driveway and on the front lawn a "FREE PARKING" sign.
A welcome mat runs down the front walk and says welcome
       in five languages.
A front door sign reads "COME IN, FREE COFFEE."
The back door is left open.

ALL TO NO AVAIL

My wife doesn't talk to me either.
She just sits there planning her next tee time, which oddly enough
       doesn't include me.
She claims that, in an effort to maintain peace and harmony in the
       community, couples are not allowed on the golf course
       together at the same time.
When we go out for dinner, we sit at different tables.
As a result, we haven't had an argument in three years, and then only
       because our tables were too close together.
A neighbor calls me once in awhile to let me know what I've done
       wrong, like I should take the American flag down whenever
       it rains. I mean, why bother to put it up? It rains every other
       day. Besides, my wife might hurt herself shinning up the tree.

Sometimes my daughter will call. I know it's my daughter because of
what I hear my wife say – "Oh, really?" "Aha," "You're
kidding," "Well I'll be," "You don't mean it," "Oh my God."
Later, when I ask my wife what's new, she'll invariably reply,
"Nothing."

I mean where have I gone wrong?
Maybe it's me.
Perhaps I need to change my ways.
Perhaps I should start by saying hello to people.
Remembering names would also help.
   "How you doin'?," just doesn't cut it in Carolina.
   Here, people expect you to remember their names.

   That's not the case in New York.
      In New York you say, "<u>How</u> ya doin'?"
      And the other party says, "How <u>you</u> doin'?"
      And that's it – conversation's over.
      You check for your wallet and move on.
But I'm here in the south, not New York.
I guess I just need to be more personable, to show interest in others,
   to ask loving, caring, thoughtful questions such as:
   • Are you still falling down a lot?
         or
   • I don't want to get personal, but is that a beauty mark on your
      chin?
Showing interest, being personable, spreading charm – that has to be the
   answer:
   • Hi, is that your real hair or are you wearing an animal?
      Being personable, showing interest – that's it!
   • Love your outfit, but isn't Halloween in October?
         or
   • Isn't it amazing what a few pounds of makeup can do?
That's the answer: showing interest, being personable, spreading
   charm.
Suddenly I feel warm and cuddly.
Ah, the joy of discovery!

A REASONABLE GUY

Look, I don't mind telling you, I'm the man of the house.
I don't do dishes, I don't do floors, and I don't cook or do wash.
I do eating and sleeping and imbibing.
I used do to sex. Now I just eat and sleep and imbibe.
I don't do shopping either.
Shopping's a woman's job, just like mowing the lawn, or changing
        a tire, or taking the garbage out.

Anyway, once in a while circumstances beyond my control compel me
        to temporarily alter my role.
Like when wife had her bladder secured.
I mean, I'm a reasonable guy, so when we ran out of cereal we flipped
        a coin to see who would go for cereal.
Actually, I was glad I lost; how do you shop with one hand holding up
        your bladder?
As I said, I'm a reasonable guy.

So I went to the supermarket.
Wife gave me a map and directions; I don't get out much anymore.
In the store I saw an aisle sign that read, cereal.
What could be easier? So I walked down the aisle.
And then it hit me (the reason I don't do shopping):
        There before me on both sides of the aisle, there jammed one
        against another for as far as I could see was every type of cereal
        ever conceived by man
                from Marshmellow Safaris & Fruity Pebbles
                to Apple Dapples and Scooby Doos,
                from Puffed Kashi and Berry Burst Cheerios
                to Honey Nut Clusters and Golden Wheat Puffs.

And that was just the first few feet.
The other side of the aisle featured
        rolls, bars, bites, tarts, chunks, and twists.
And all I wanted was a small box of Rice Krispies!
I tried, I really did.

I searched over and across, up and down, back and forth.
After twenty minutes, I found myself talking to the cereal boxes.
Long forgotten obscenities spewed from my lips, clearing the area
of other lost souls.
Suddenly, I realized I was alone and unarmed.
I had to get out of there.
As I ran out of the store to the safety of my car, I vowed from that
moment on I would only eat eggs for breakfast.
I mean, how many varieties of eggs could there be?

When I returned home, I propped wife up and told her the store had
run out of Rice Krispies.

She smiled understandingly, and I think it was at that moment that we
both realized that I would never again go shopping, not for
Rice Krispies or anything else, that I would rather eat the daily
newspaper than once again walk down an aisle from hell.

EPILOGUE

Wife's bladder was successfully secured, and she once again does
all the shopping.
Marital bliss has returned and happiness is again ours.

Makes a nice Christmas story!

It All Matters

WHAT IS THIS THING CALLED RAP?

I'm into classical, myself.
You know, the old guys: Mozart, Brahms, Bach, Beethoven, Haydn,
        Strauss, Tchaikovsky, all of whom brought us music that
        delighted the senses and stimulated the intellect.
I also enjoyed the many melodies of the '40s and '50s.
And for the same melodic reason, I enjoyed at least some of the music
        of the '60s, '70s, and even the '80s.
There was always melody.
Music you could sing to – like
    "How much is that doggie in the window, the one with the
    waggely tail?"
 or "Pardon me boys, is that the Chattanogga Choo Choo, Track 29?"
    – one as great as the next.
And who could forget –
    "Mairzy doats and dozey doats and liddle lamzy divey, a kiddly
    divey too, wouldn't you?"
    Even the lyrics were great.

And what do we have today?
What is it?
It can't be music. If it is, we're doomed.
We have gone from concertos and fugues and melodies to what we
        have today.
I think they call it rap.
I don't mean to be nasty, but if I need a laxative, I'll go to the
        drug store.
What is "rap?" Can you hum it? Can you sing it?
Can you remember it? Can you even understand it?
Or do you sit there in awe and wonder what's happening?
What's really scary is to project what we have today ten years
        down the road.
We'll be back to the Neanderthal days.
Grunts and farts that's what we'll hear.
That's the direction we're going in.
No melodies, no concertos, sonatas, or fugues, just grunts and farts.
And you know the kids will love it.

They'll sit there with their rainbow colored hair and body piercing and
    grunt and fart and wonder why we're not doing the same.

Amadeus, Johann, Wolfgang, Irving, Ira, Cole, Sammy, where are you?
For the sake of civilized man, come back!
I'm too old to hunt for food, and I'm certainly too old to wear
    a loin cloth.
Come back, Oh, Masters of Melody.
Entertain us with your music,
    Come back, Oh, "Chattanooga Choo Choo."
    Come back, Oh, "Doggie in the Window."
Come back concertos, sonatas, and fugues.
Return and save us from:
    this gluttony of garble,
    this deluge of dribble,
    this ritual of rambling,
    this tumult of trash,
    this thing they call rap.

THE BARGAIN

It was the spring of the year.
I had bought a pair of cargo shorts at Sam's.
I like Sam's. I like the free food. You know, the samples.
Sometimes, I'll even bring along a disguise so I can get seconds.
Anyway, the shorts were of good color, lots of pockets, a great price,
      and as a New Yorker would say, "a real bargain."
When I got home, I tried them on.
Instead of a zipper in the front, there was, to my utter astonishment,
      a button, one single button in the middle of a 3-inch opening.
Without getting too personal, let me just say, "No way."
And, believe me, I tried every conceivable approach: left, right, up,
      down.
You can only stretch it so far, you know.
Nothing worked.
I even tried standing on my head. Also jumping jacks and
      pelvis thrusts.
There was no denying it: the little guy was a prisoner of Sam's.
Oh, the horror of it all!

Too lazy to return them and too frugal to throw them out, I wore
      them even though finding relief required me to pull them
      down around my knees.
This caused no additional problems at home, as Elaine would always
      run out of the house whenever I pulled my pants down.
      It did, however, cause quite a stir in the local men's room. Many
found it unsettling and left. Still others
      stayed and introduced themselves.
      – And yes, I kept a list.
While I appreciate the host of new acquaintances I made in my
      one-button shorts and the many dinner invitations I received,
      and while I'll miss the adoration of the numerous groupies,
      despite all this, I think from now on I'll let Elaine
      pick out my pants for me. I mean, at my age, who needs to be
      the most popular guy in town?

THE PREDICAMENT

Please be forewarned: the following subject material is of a frank,
personal nature.
So, if you are at all squeamish, you might consider putting your head
back, closing your eyes, and doing what you usually do –
pretend you're a ballerina.
It's OK, big guy; it's a liberal world.

Now for the tale.

I'll never forget the sheer terror of that day. I had just finished
answering nature's call.
I mean the "real" thing, the "main event," when I realized to my utter
horror that there were no wipes on the spool, nor were there
any in sight.
Oh, the horror of it all! What to do? Drying takes forever. I
considered a nearby towel, but how do I explain to Elaine?
Remember, she's Italian, and I'm allergic to knives.
To make matters worse, our bathroom faces the ninth tee, and at
Elaine's insistence, our blinds are drawn at half-mast.
Yes, you can see in. What to do?

The answer came slowly, painfully:
- crawl and find the back up supply
- crawl on all fours and pray that no one sees me
- most of all, pray that there will be no "danglers"
Oh, the sheer horror of it all!
I don't think anyone did see me, but now I cringe whenever I hear the
expression, "bottoms up," and I have to wonder what they're
talking about.

The good news is that there are preventative measures.
First of – carry a roll of wipes wherever you go:
- yes, even in your golf bag,
- definitely in your auto,
- and, if you carry one, in your purse.

It All Matters

Secondly – equip your bathroom with a handy, reachable, yet
plentiful back up supply.
    – there is absolutely nothing wrong with piling them
    up in the most accessible corner.

There is one other thing you can do.
Whenever the call comes, when it's time for the real thing,
    go to your neighbors.
This way, if you run into an empty spool, and you're caught in the act
    of retrieving, the viewer will think it's your neighbor.
Better to be called a lousy neighbor than a pervert.

THE LAST LAUGH

This tale of horror takes place in the bedroom. At the time, I was lying
   in bed reading, which is usually what I do in bed now.

Anyway, I was trying to finish a chapter. It was late, and I was getting
   nervous.
My wife, Elaine, had planned a busy next day for me. She wanted me
   to dust. In our house, dusting is a labor-intensive, all day job.
   If you're Italian you'll understand. If you're not, ask an Italian.
Just don't ask when they're dusting unless you like to dust.
Anyway, out of nowhere I heard it – BZZ—BZZ—BZZ.
   Yes, it was a fly.
I could tell it was a big fly – no little fly makes that much noise. He
   made another pass –BZZ—BZZ—BZZ. This was a serious fly
   out for no good.
I knew I had to get it before it got me. So I carefully sneaked out of
   the room and armed myself with my favorite fly swatter. It was
   a Father's Day gift from Sam's. My kids always go all out for
   Father's Day. I was ready for battle. I slowly examined the
   walls, the ceiling, the carpet – no fly. I made the same
   careful inspection of the bathroom – nothing.
It was now 1:00 a.m., and I felt my anxiety soaring. All I could think of
   was being too tired to dust the next day. And then I saw him. I
   knew it was "HIM," because he was very large, hairy, and
   muscular. No "SHE" would ever let herself go like that.
   He was sitting on my nightshirt on the floor. The fool
   probably thought I was in it. It was comforting to know he
   wasn't too bright.
   I approached slowly, deliberately.
   I aimed, swung, and I nailed him.
I hit him again and again. I want you to know I beat the
   "fly" out of him!
And in triumphant mood, I grabbed some tissue and threw him in the
   toilet like some old "discarded" fly. Then I turned the lights
   out and crawled into bed. And then it came to me, a terrifying

thought. Maybe he was just pretending. Maybe he could swim.
Worst of all, maybe he had a family.
So I seized the moment, jumped out of bed, and I FLUSHED!

You're probably wondering where Elaine was all this time. She had
  feigned restlessness and had sought sanctuary in another part
  of the house. I thought nothing of it at the time, but later my
  suspicions grew.
 How, I thought, could someone who falls asleep during sex suddenly
  become restless?
The next day I made no mention of my struggle.
But that night I feigned restlessness and moved to another part of the
  house – leaving behind a big, hairy, muscular fly.
It might have been the father.
As I fell asleep, I could not help but hear her cries of anguish.

Some tales have a happy ending.

THE VISITATION

My knee had recently been operated on, and, with the help of some
crutches, I was counting the weeds in my back yard. I used to
do crossword puzzles, but then they started using five and six
letter words. Counting weeds is easier. I count up to ten and
then start over. Education is a wonderful thing!

But let's get back to our tale.

Suddenly, I noticed a stranger approaching from a nearby tee. His gate
was slow yet certain. His face was calm yet determined. His
beard was shaggy, yet somehow appropriate. I hardly knew what
to expect.

The stranger walked right up to me and asked, "Do you believe in
God?"

"I do," I replied.

He then asked, "Would you pray with me?"

What was I going to say? "No, I have weeds to count."

So we prayed. Actually he prayed, and I stood there with my head
bowed and my eyes open, expecting I knew not what.
His prayer was short and to the point. He asked that my injury
heal quickly, and that I be allowed to return to an exciting,
productive life. He obviously didn't know I was retired.
Anyway, the prayer ended, and we stood there looking at each
other. I didn't know what to do. So I did the only thing I could
think of. I dropped my crutches, looked up to the heavens
and cried, "I'm cured!" The visitor said nothing. He just
walked back to the tee, picked up his club, and swung.
The ball landed on the green some 500 yards away.
It was only then that I noticed his club.
It had a peculiar shape to it.

By God, it wasn't a club at all; it was a staff. And those weren't people
with him; they were sheep. And those weren't "boos" I had
heard; they were "baas."

Two lingering questions remain:
        *** Does God play golf?
    and ***Does God have a sense of humor?

122

It All Matters

I really don't care about the first question.
I mean, if God plays golf, that's fine with me.
I mean, what are a few more miracles here or there:
      *** like a hole in less than one?
  or *** never missing a three-foot putt?
  or *** never having to walk around water?

And that's all OK.
But it's the second question that concerns me. Does God have a sense
     of humor?
I'd feel a whole lot better about the whole thing if He had smiled
     when I dropped my crutches. But there was no smile.
     The corners of His mouth went down.
     I mean down as in frown. And when He walked away,
     I noticed some writing on the back of His robe. It read,
     "Have a nice trip, and bring plenty of sun tan lotion with you."

See, He does have a sense of humor!   Right?

FLOG

I picked up the following descriptive passages somewhere
and changed most only slightly:

1. Golf can best be described as a continuous series of
   mishaps compensated for by occasional divine intervention.

2. Golf is a hard game to figure:
   > One day you'll go out and top it, slice it, pull it,
   > shank it, lose it, hit in traps, miss every green,
   > and three putt every hole, and then the next day
   > you'll go out and for no reason at all,
   > you'll really stink.

3. You know why they call it golf, don't you?
   > All the other four letter words were taken,
   > like "oops," "help," "oofa," and although
   > five letters long, "angst" would have been appropriate.
   > But personally, I prefer FLOG.
   > FLOG says it all.
   > FLOG has a certain ring to it.
   > Hey buddy, you want to go FLOGGING?

4. Anyway, if you find you enjoy FLOGGING in the wind
   > and rain or in the heat and humidity,
   > or if you enjoy playing while your body hosts every
   > insect known to man, here's a tip for you:
   > you're sick and you need help.

5. But I think it was a fellow golfer who said it best:
   > He said, and I quote,
   > "I quit my job to get stress out of my life,
   > and then I took up golf."

It All Matters

Know that golf is a game of contradictions:

- You swing easy to make it go far.
- You hit down on the ball to make it go up.
- You maximize your weak side and minimize
  your strong side.
- You are to relax and have confidence in your ability,
  even though you're twitching and have no ability.
- You are to socialize, meet people, and make friends,
  but don't talk to anyone while they're playing.
- And most contradictory of all,
  the lowest score wins.

Oh, there's more!

Golf is so designed to equalize abilities.
This equalizer is called a handicap, and everybody has one.
And the worse you are, the more of a handicap you get,
      sort of a reward for inability.
Applying this same logic to other sports:

- the best prizefighters would use only one hand,
- the best baseball players would hit with a broom stick,
- and the best fullbacks would be limited to a hop and
  a skip.

This way all competitive levels and leagues could be eliminated.
And anyone could best anyone else on any given day, regardless of
ability.
If you're lousy, what's not to like?

But let's move on. There's more to golf than contradictions.

Did you ever wonder why some drivers are so large
      and others so small?
That's because the large ones have motors in them.
I played with a guy recently who asked me to help
      him carry his club to the tee.
When I declined, he attached wheels and
      rolled it to the tee himself.
Then he asked me to help him swing it.
When I again declined, he pulled a chain
      of some sort and started it up.

125

Unfortunately for him, it stalled halfway though his swing,
    and he knocked himself out.
We don't play together anymore, and I understand
    his golf attire now includes a helmet.

Speaking of swings, did you ever observe a golfer
    immediately after his or her swing?
    Easy to tell when a good strike has been made:
- the individual poses –
    head up, eyes straight ahead,
    body perfectly still and leaning forward,
    as if to say, "Go ahead, take my picture."
Just as easy to identify is when a poor strike has been made:
- now anger, dismay, and disgust take over,
    and posing is replaced by action –
    a dejected nod of the head, a shrug
    of the shoulders, a wave of the hand,
    a kick of the foot, any of which
    might well be accompanied by a few
    well-chosen expletives.
    In the rarest of cases, action might also take
    the form of club banging or even tossing.
    Fortunately, these cases are extremely rare,
    and any use of protective gear on the
    golf course remains strictly voluntary.

I really don't know if golf is for me:
- I remember the time I approached the tee,
    took my practice swing and waggle, and realized
    there was no ball on the tee.
    I swung anyway.
    My partner said it was the best drive I had all day.
    I never did like him.
- Or the time I set a tee time for my group
    and unintentionally left myself out.
    The group asked me to make the same

arrangements next week.
> I never liked any of them.

- Once, I put the ball in the club washer and left without
  a ball and a dirty club.
- Wife got me a pail and shovel for the sand traps.
  She figured they'd be as productive
  as my sand wedge and a lot more fun.
- She also got me some scuba equipment, claiming the
  sighting of alligators was just idle talk.
- What's really upsetting, though,
  is when eleven-year-olds ask to play through.
  Maybe next time I'll offer them my scuba equipment.

Only cheating keeps me going.
You know, to even things out.
Well, you believe in the handicap system, don't you?
Well, cheating is my handicap, my equalizer.

Here are a few of my favorites:

- Wear camouflaged shoes and pants,
  – This way no one will see you
  when you improve the lie.
- Never put a personal ID marker on your ball.
  – This way you can say the ball found
  in the woods is not yours.
- Ignore the out of bounds markers.
  – If you can play it, hit it,
  and if you can't play it, move it.
  And remember, there is nothing
  better to hit off of than a neatly
  manicured lawn.
- Carry plenty of balls with you at all times.
  – This way if you lose a ball,
  you can always find it again.
- If you hit a ball in the trap, step on it.
  – This way you can find it again
  on the green.

   – And if that's not practical to do,
   stoop way down and throw the ball out.
   Calling attention to a passing tornado
   or flying saucer will serve to distract
   the other players.
*   Always limp and wear visible support bandages.
   – The more bandages you wear, the more of a
   handicap you can request.
   Limping also helps, but hysterics are the best.
   Who wants to argue with a crying, out-of-control grownup?
*   Whenever possible play by yourself and keep your own score.
   – This way you can post what you should have scored.
*   And finally and most importantly,
   learn to swear in at least two obscure languages.
   – This way when you lose control,
   you can say anything you want.

And that's as much as I can help you.
   I'll see you on the links.
   Look for me.
   I'm easy to find. I wear a raincoat,
         and I'm usually in the woods.
But that doesn't matter.
   What does matter is that I'll be out there tomorrow,
   and the day after, and the day after that,
   swinging away, giving it my all,
   dreaming the impossible dream –
   that I'm a golfer.
I know you'll be out there, too.
I know you share my dream.
And so good luck, good FLOGGING, and remember,
   if at first you don't succeed,
   try, try again.
   There's always a miracle just waiting to happen.

GOOD MORNING

I attend church most Sunday mornings. Well, more often than not.
    All right, once in a while.
Anyway, there's a part of every service where the congregation greets
    his or her neighbor. And so for what seems like forever,
    everyone can be seen spinning and turning and smiling and
    saying – GOOD MORNING, GOOD MORNING,
    GOOD MORNING.
I'm sitting there with indigestion from the night before, and they're
    wishing me a cheerful GOOD MORNING. I want to die,
    and they want to play missionary. Please, not everyone stays
    home on a Saturday night and has tea and crumpets. I mean, if
    they really cared, they'd leave me alone or offer me a bicarb,
    or at least change their greeting to something more
    appropriate, like CHEERS or BOTTOMS UP.
    On second thought, make that alternative greeting,
    GOOD LUCK.

At any rate, the situation became unbearable, and so one Sunday I was
    determined to initiate a change, to replace GOOD
    MORNING with something more suitable to my disposition
    and state of mind. And so at the next service, when
    this prim and proper lady turned around and said, GOOD
    MORNING to me, I replied, <u>HOW</u> YA DOIN'? It was
    like she didn't hear me. She just continued spinning, turning,
    and saying GOOD MORNING, GOOD MORNING.
    I tried changing inflection, I said, HOW <u>YOU</u> DOIN'?
    I even tried HOW YOU <u>DOIN'</u>? Nothing, nothing worked.
    Every Sunday, GOOD MORNING echoed through out the
    church.

And then finally, a few services later, I at long last received the
    response I had worked and waited for so long. Some wise and
    noble gentleman answered my <u>HOW</u> YA DOIN'? with a
    HOW <u>YOU</u> DOIN'?
It was wonderful. I get goose bumps just thinking about it.

Unfortunately, I couldn't handle the success, and regrettably
   replied, YOU DON'T WANT TO KNOW. The wise,
   noble gentleman just spun around and reverted back to
   GOOD MORNING.– I had blown it.

Now when I go to church and the time for GOOD MORNING
   arrives, I just close my eyes hoping they'll pass me by. As a last
   resort, I'll nod my head up and down.
Maybe the nod will catch on.
I mean, I could live with a nod; you wouldn't have to speak, and no
   one would know what you were thinking. Can't you just see it?
      – an entire congregation spinning, and turning, and smiling,
      and nodding their heads.
I'm getting goose bumps again.

HOLIDAY GREETINGS

Dec. 25, 2000

Hi,

It's "Easy Al" with a few words of joy for everyone. I know you
love these group letters, but I've grown old and lazy. So here's
our update for the previous 12 months.

In December '99, going home for Christmas we totaled our car. It was
my wife's way of getting a new one.
The important thing is that we're alive and well, and pretty soon I'll be
out of this body cast. See, there's joy in everything.

In February '00, I had my knee operated on, a combined result of old
age and Elaine's driving. But that's fair;
Elaine got a new car, and I got a repaired knee.

In March, I passed out in church and saw the face of God. Let me tell
you, it wasn't Bill Clinton. Nothing serious, but now I pray at
home.

Not to be outdone, in August Elaine had some female problems
attended to. I don't know what that means either. I will tell
you, however, that the problem was not the result of an
overactive sex life, not in the last 31 years, anyway.
Her favorite expression is "don't touch me."
It's really OK, because at this point in my life, I wouldn't know what
with. It's called sexual compatibility. So we're happy!

Each morning we check our bodies for new growths. What was once
a simple pimple, now requires a biopsy. I look forward to this
time, however, because it's the only time I get to see her;
usually she's wrapped up in an overcoat. The remainder of the
a.m. is spent trying to stand up, and on a good day, walk.
Bending is a memory.

Afternoons are filled with golf and stained glass. If it gets more
exciting, I'll probably pass out again. But the highlight of the

day is the cocktail hour. To me the day begins at 5:00 p.m.
For one hour, I become the "Easy Al" you know and
remember. All is well with the world. Life is good.
People are good.

And dinner is good, although we eat out a lot now, as Elaine claims the
new kitchen is too large. Fox News and the O'Reilly Factor fill most
evenings and by 9:00 p.m. I'm ready to declare my candidacy.

By 10:00 p.m., I revive Elaine and put her to bed. It's usually at this time
that she softly whispers into my ear, "Don't touch me," and as I indicated
before, it's just as well.

Time for you to open up your other cards. So, on behalf of Elaine,
who is all the world to me, and "Easy Al", we wish
you and yours the happiest of times.

ON KEEPING IT SIMPLE

A few words regarding the new technology of the 21st century.
Let's start with what was once Ford's "baby," the automobile,
  and see how manufacturers today, while adding
  convenience and beauty, are at the same time
  threatening our sanity.

What comes to mind first is the handy, little remote control.
You know, the little two-by-two inch magic box:
  the one with the hieroglyphics,
  the one that allows you to remotely
  open and lock the door and open the trunk.
There's also a separate button that sets off a siren
  of such magnitude that it might well cause
  one to seek shelter.
The fun starts when you try to identify the desired button.
Your only guide is a set of miniature symbols
  that challenge both your vision
  and your interpretive powers.
All I can tell you is that I spend a lot of time
  opening and closing the trunk,
  opening and locking the doors,
  and hysterically seeking a way to stifle the damn siren.
And then there's the new high tech safety lock for the back doors.
While its intended purpose may be to safeguard
  the immature in the rear, it also
  does a damn fine job of bringing the driver
  a step closer to seeking psychiatric help.
I mean, I get out of the driver's seat
  to fetch something out of the back,
  only to find that the back door is locked.
I didn't lock it. It was open before, and now it's locked.
So I take the little magic box,
  push a button, whose hieroglyphics I can't read,
  or understand, and the trunk opens.
I then physically close the trunk.

I push another button and the siren goes off.
Now bystanders are staring at me.
So I panic and push all the buttons:

> – the trunk reopens,

> – the siren shuts down,

> – and the back door opens.

Two out of three's not bad!

Oh, there's more:
High tech has also brought Ford's "baby"
> a new high-styled, attractive, design-integrated,

> totally useless, functionless bumper – front and back.

Do not, under any circumstances, strike anything
> with your new high-styled, attractive,
> design-integrated bumper.

Do not tap, touch, or God forbid, strike anything
> of substance with your bumper; for it is so constructed as to
> either crumble, dent, chip, crack, or disappear upon impact.

And then, of course, it's off to your friendly
> body repair shop for an estimate that
> will invariably come in below your deductible.

It gets worse:
Would you believe TV monitors in autos?
This way when a driver gets bored with watching the road,
> or conversing with his family, he need only pop in a
> DVD and watch a movie.

And the kids can continue to feed their escape from reality with
> a variety of programs designed to stunt mental growth.

And worse:
This latest "marvel," direct from a black hole somewhere, is a
> navigation system, which tells the driver step-by-step, turn-by-
> turn, direction-by-direction, how to get wherever he/she wants
> to go, thus eliminating the need for memory, a map, a sense of
> direction, or even a friendly gas station attendant.

Should you find this to be an exaggeration, go along with it anyway,

for what may be an exaggeration today, will surely be an
understatement tomorrow.

I mean, there are absolutely no limits to the "marvels" of the 21st
century, and it should come as no surprise if next week's
innovation made the drivers' only requirement to whisper the
destination to the steering wheel.

Just give the destination, and then sit back, enjoy the TV, play some
video games, read a book, do some crocheting, and leave the
driving to man's latest "marvel."

Like the Neanderthals, we are doomed.

Oh, for the "ole" Ford with the big, strong, shinny, functional
bumpers, the push-pull door locks, the trunk that requires
a key to open, a source of entertainment limited to the radio,
or, God forbid, the passengers themselves, and a driver
capable of thinking and reaching a destination all by
him or herself.

And best of all – no siren.

Just the peace and comfort that comes with simplicity.

Well, I can dream, can't I?

HELP !

Went shopping the other day.
Not that I like to go shopping, but
       it was time to update my high tech equipment.
So I checked the sale ads in the paper and off I went.

First stop was for a TV.
Mine wasn't working well.
      One rabbit ear was broken, and
    the scotch tape wasn't holding anymore.
The salesman explained that there were basically 3 types:
        1.   High Definition Digital
            with – 2-Tuner PIP, Progressive Scan,
                  Dolby Virtual & Universal Remote Control
        2.   Wide Screen Projection HDTV
            with – MTS Stereo/SAP, Twinview 2- Tuner PIP,
                  Tru surround SRS Audio Dolby
                  Digital Comfort
        3.   Plasma EDTVs and ADTs
            with – Wide screen Plasma Monitor
                  3000:1 Contrast Ratio,
                  Split Screen PIP,
                  SRS Tru Surround XT,
                  Speakers and Pedestal Stand
I was thankful for the Speakers and Pedestal Stand,
      for those were the only items I recognized.
Anyway, he went on for a good fifteen minutes,
      as though a switch had been turned on.
Whenever he came up for air, I tried to explain
      that all I wanted was a 12 inch black-and-white TV
      with two dials: one for volume and the other for channels,
      like the one my father had given me.
After a while, the salesman started to shake,
      and shortly thereafter he excused himself.
Something about a lunch break,
      but I don't think he felt too well.

It All Matters

Anyway, he left and I treated myself
      to a brand new set of rabbit ears and
      moved on to the camera department.
It was time to replace my Brownie automatic.
Not because it didn't work, but because people kept staring, and
      I like to keep a low profile.

Hundreds of lenses and one salesman greeted me
      as I entered the camera department.
It was Yogi's, "déjà vu all over again"
      with digitals, zooms, opticals, swivelscrews,
      monitors, and of course,
      a vast range of megapixels.
I tried to stop him, I really did.
I told the salesman I wasn't looking for a "digit,"
      but rather a camera, specifically a Brownie automatic,
      with a "pop-in" flash bulb.
It was like he didn't hear me,
      and by now I was convinced that the two salesmen
      were either related or very good friends.
I thought that because when I told him again
      that all I wanted was a new Brownie,
      he started shaking and excused himself, just like the
      other salesman.
Anyway, I couldn't find a Brownie automatic,
      so I bought some film and went to lunch.
There was, after all, nothing wrong with my father's camera.

On my way out, I noticed a woman talking to the palm of her hand.
I followed her for a while fearing for her well being
      and then realized she was holding something.
Closer examination revealed a type of phone,
      and she appeared to be carrying on a conversation.
Suddenly she stopped talking and
      to my utter astonishment,
      aimed this same phone at some innocent child.
If I didn't know better, I would have sworn
      she had taken the child's picture.

Now it was my turn to start shaking,
     and I knew it was time to go home.
Anyway, I was content with my father's rotary phone
     and needed time to update my 12 inch black-and-white TV
     with the new rabbit ears.
My favorite program, The Lawrence Welk Show, would be on later,
     and I didn't want to miss that.
Besides, I had done enough "updating" for one day.

CASUAL AND COMFORTABLE

Simply put, I hate shopping, the whole nine yards:
> from the beginning to the end,
> from the time it takes to get there,
> to the traffic you have to fight through,
> to the sales assistance that isn't,
> to the money you impulsively spend,
> to the waiting for others to finish,
> to the better part of a day lost.

Allow me to tell you about two recent shopping ventures.
My wife and I had recently visited our in-laws.
After a few totally enjoyable days of R & R,
> wife decided I needed a new pair of shoes,
> something casual, something comfortable.

And so accompanied by my daughter-in-law,
> an avid shopper, and her father,
> a saintly man of high intellect,
> we set out for the area's shopping haven,
> ten miles of back-to-back stores, accompanied by
> ten miles of back-to-back traffic.

Our son had stayed back:
> − something about a headache

> − a maneuver he had learned from his mother
> > with regard to an entirely different matter.

Surprisingly, we arrived on the same day
> at what was described by locals,
> as the world's largest warehouse shoe outlet.

It did have shoes, a lot of shoes, as far as you could see, shoes.
Unfortunately, the inventory was sexist in nature
> with eight aisles devoted to the female foot
> and two to the male.

In case math's not your thing,
> that would make woman four times more important than man.
> And I thought the ratio was two to one!

To further add to my frustration, there was no sales help,

139

and each aisle offered but one "fitting" chair,
and one shoe horn.
I would have rather shopped for Rice Krispies.

It took but one pass through to realize
that my casual, comfortable shoes were not to be,
not here anyway, and so I retreated
back to the car to await the girls.
Father-in-law, always the wise one, never left the car.
He had been down this road before
and was content playing with his new road mate
navigation system, which, thanks to a gal named Agnes
with a voice like Marilyn,
provided at the very least, detailed travel instructions.
Had I known about Agnes with a voice like Marilyn,
I never would have left the car.
Who wants to shop when you can fantasize?
I mean she, Agnes, was something else.
You might say, she was capable of warming the
cockles of one's heart.
  On the other hand, you might not say that at all.
Anyway, at this point, there were two men in the car,
one with patience, the other with angst,
both waiting for the shoppers, two women
armed with multiple credit cards.
After thirty minutes of calling on God for strength,
wife appeared as if from heaven
and proceeded to tell us in great detail
of her "absolute steals" of the day.
Translation: three more entries for our two-page list of monthly
charges.
Now we were three waiting in the car for my daughter-in-law,
who loves shopping more that life itself.
And she didn't disappoint.
Some forty-five minutes later she appeared with selections
from aisles three through ten.
Claiming to have saved a small fortune,
she extended dinner invitations to all.
Feeling entitled, I accepted.

It All Matters

Things were looking up.

There was only one thing missing –
I didn't have my new casual, comfortable shoes,
        which, I reminded the girls,
        was the original purpose of our trip.
So off we went again back into the ten miles of traffic.
God is merciful, and before long we stumbled upon
        this little shoe store in the corner of this
        little shopping center.
It couldn't have been as large as the
        men's room in the warehouse store.
Not knowing what to expect, we entered.
A woman with something wrapped around her entire body greeted us.
Wife informed me it was a sari.
I thought she said she was sorry, and I suggested that
        as long as we were there, we should make the most of it.
Wife just stared at me as only she can.
Anyway, we couldn't have been in the store
        a minute, when I spotted another woman,
        also wearing a sari, scurrying out the back.
There was also a baby in a port-a-crib on the floor,
        who insisted on staring at me with the largest,
        darkest, most penetrating eyes I had ever seen.
As discreetly as I could,
        I looked for the nearest exit.
But before I could accomplish this, the first sari asked
        if she could be of assistance.
        And those were her exact words,
        "May I be of assistance?"
Someone was actually trying to help me.
My first impulse was to shower her with affection,
        at least a hug anyway,
        but fearing I might offend, as is usually the case
        when I offer affection, I did nothing.
As it turned out the sari was a lady,
        who spoke better English than anyone of us.
She was bright, knowledgeable, and able,

141

actually listening to my needs, and then
    quickly steering me to exactly what I had in mind.
She also managed to upgrade me to a second,
    more expensive pair of shoes, again casual and comfortable,
    along with several pairs of socks.
Not to be outdone, wife picked out a pair she "just had to have,"
    making the score 4 to 2,
    and assuring her of yet another shopping triumph.
So everyone was happy:

- money is for spending, or so I've been instructed,
- the expedition took only half a day,
- the girls added to their shoe collections,
- and I had my two pairs of shoes, casual and comfortable.

Even Agnes cooperated and navigated us safely home.
I suddenly found myself in a rare Thanksgiving mood. I had
    survived yet another shopping expedition,
    defying the odds, lasting the day, while maintaining my sanity.

Unfortunately, my joy was short-lived,
    for the very next morning wife informed me
    that I was now in need of casual and comfortable
    slacks and shirts to complement
    my new casual and comfortable shoes.
My only consolation, which I gloated over and kept to myself,
    was the knowledge that my underwear was already
    casual and comfortable.
Translation: just one more shopping day – and done,
    at least on this trip, anyway.

A CRY FOR SOCIALIZED PACKAGING

There is little doubt that today's packaging calls for an in depth
investigation.
It doesn't matter what product, or what manufacturer.
Packaging today is so designed to encourage disposal after first
opening, for to re-close or reseal requires a skill and
temperament beyond the capabilities of modern man.
"Resealable Pouch"—Really!
The label says, "Cut Here" and you do, but too high,
and so you still can't open the package.
So you cut again.
This time too low and now your "Reusable Pouch"
is about as useful as a pouch on a sterile kangaroo.
If producers are so concerned about freshness,
why don't they just enclose a clip in each package?
You know, some inexpensive, plastic, all purpose, throw away
clip.
In addition to assuring the freshness of the product,
a clip would most assuredly preserve the sanity
and increase the life span of the average consumer.

Standard, uniform packaging. That's what we need!
Simple, easy, all the same packaging,
requiring no more than a high school education
to open and close. That's it!
And if this be a step towards "socialized packaging,"
so be it.

There's more to the packaging problem, much more.
Some producers insist on fusing closed their product
with a heavy-duty plastic, plastic so thick and strong
it could easily be used to protect a house from
storm damage.
Such a protective wrapping is not a problem until one attempts
to free the package contents.
Then the protective wrapping becomes a nearly impenetrable

shield.
Allow me to save you some angst.
In such a case, go directly for the sharpest instrument you can
        find, like a knife or an awl, and unmercifully attack it.

You'll feel a whole lot better for your efforts,
        and eventually, if you don't injure yourself,
        you'll free the "prisoner."

Not a bad idea to have a tourniquet
        and a supply of bandages handy.
Preparation is everything.

And how about those lightweight cartons
        that carry a lightweight load,
        like cereal for example?
While scores of nutritional facts clutter each side of the carton,
        there are, in most cases, no instructions
        on how to open the carton.
So you proceed on your own. I mean, how difficult can it be?
        It's cardboard.
You see a tab, or what looks like a tab,
        and you pull.
Far too frequently this proves to be the bottom of the carton,
        leaving you with a damaged, still unopened,
        lightweight carton.

Now, it's true that some lightweight packages
        make an effort at posting instructions:

TO OPEN SLIDE FINGER
UNDER TAB AND BREAK SEAL
LEFT TO RIGHT

Mind you, not RIGHT TO LEFT – LEFT TO RIGHT.
Like, what would happen if you went the wrong way?
Would it implode?
But let's assume you got the message right and went the

correct way.
In all probability, you'll wind up with the tab in your hand
and the carton still sealed.
Probably something to do with improper placement or
quality of glue, and a tab so designed
as to serve no purpose at all.
Anyway, at this point you've lost control and find yourself
clawing at anything resembling a tab.
And you succeed.

Not only do you eventually succeed in opening the carton,
you succeed in removing the entire top portion of the
carton.
Desperate to go on with your life, you pick up what was once
the top of the carton and read the closing instructions:
INSERT TAB HERE

I know of only one place where I'd like to insert the tab.

THE PRICE YOU PAY

You're half awake.
It's 3:00 a.m. and your stomach tells you that
      you've been a bad boy.
You need some of that soothing pink stuff.
So you stumble to the bathroom and without
      turning on the light, you feel for the bottle.
God is good and after a few fumbling moments, you find it.
Your fingers immediately tell you that this is no ordinary bottle, and
      that the top is fused in a type of plastic that will require more
      than a finger nail to remove.
You settle for the only instrument you can find – a pair of scissors –
      and after several minutes of probing and stabbing,
      you break the plastic shield.
Now all that remains is to unscrew the cap.
So you twist, and then you twist again,
      and then you reverse twist – nothing.
Nothing because it is one of these 21st century safety "marvels,"
      that requires either a gorilla or mechanical engineer to open.
You decide a closer investigation is needed, along with a light.
      So you flip the switch and then wait for your pupils to adjust.
AH! – two grooves and an arrow.
What could be simpler? Squeeze the groves
      and turn the cap in the direction of the arrow.
After a few practice runs and satisfied that you have correctly
      coordinated the two steps, you turn the cap.
You've done it! Victory is yours!!
Something, however, reminds you that the pink stuff
      requires vigorous shaking before using.
So you vigorously shake.
You stop only upon observing that your once
      mint green walls now run with the color pink.
A strict religious upbringing takes over
      and you brush aside the unthinkable,
      that God has forsaken you.
      And in an effort to preserve your marriage,
      you clean up the mess.

It All Matters

Perhaps a pain-relieving pill will do just as well.
Here all that is required is a simple push and turn;
  the bottle having been opened several days ago,
  the war won after a prolonged attack with an awl,
  the shreds of aluminum foil removed piece by piece.

So you confidently turn the cap and then watch
  as hundreds of little white tablets fall to the floor.
You grab a couple on the way down,
  throw them into your mouth
  and swallow without water.
You're playing it safe now,
  for the quest for water would necessitate
  another episode of "turning," and just the thought
  of that is more than you can bear.
Eventually the little tablets go down,
  and you return to bed fully awake,
  accompanied by a terrible taste in your mouth,
  a pounding in your ears,
  and a stomach that promises never to forgive you.

Sometimes there's a price to pay for safety.
Sometimes you wonder if the price is worth the benefit.

ON BECOMING A RECLUSE

For most retirees one of the highlights of each day is fetching
     the mail.
Both the excitement of the trip and the quest for continued solvency
     make that true.
The other highlight, far exceeding the first, is the cocktail "hour,"
     usually beginning at 5:00 p.m. and ending sometime
     between 7:00 and 8:00 p.m.
 But let's save that for another time.
This is about the mail, its contents, and its packaging.
Along with thirteen catalogues, three credit card solicitations,
     one coupon savings offer, and one retiree announcement,
     today's delivery brought two additional envelopes.
Both were bills.
After fifty years you just know.
What I couldn't determine was how to open them.

The first one had no unglued edge or flap to grab on to.
The envelope was sealed tight.
I mean tight; edge to edge and flap to flap as if
     to offer a challenge on how to open it.
After a few failed attempts at breaking the seal,
     the attack shifted to the envelope's short end.
In a very few seconds the short end
     along with a portion of the envelope's contents were shredded.
There are times that try man's soul.
     Like now.

Incredulously, the challenge of opening this first envelope
     would be dwarfed by the efforts required
     to open the second.
For before me lay the new, all improved, multipurpose,
     "wonder" envelope of the 21st century.
It appeared considerably larger than the old,
     now outdated business envelope I was accustomed to.

It All Matters

A closer look indicated that the printing on both sides
        of the envelope listed opening instructions,
        clearly indicating that a proper opening
        sequence needed to be followed:

TEAR BOTH SIDES FIRST
BEND BEFORE TEARING
TEAR TOP BACK FLAP ONLY AFTER
        TEARING BOTH SIDES
PULL TAB ONLY AFTER
        TEARING BOTH SIDES
        AND TOP BACK FLAP

I tried, I really did,
        but my degree is in liberal arts, not engineering.
So rather than destroy another bill,
        I brought the "wonder" envelope over to my neighbor,
        an engineer of reputable standing.
After careful analysis, and repeated use of his slide rule,
        my engineer friend of reputable standing
        opened the envelope and then proceeded
        to explain how this 21st century innovation
        could also be used as a return envelope.
How could it get better than this?
Anyway, problem solved,
        unless of course my neighbor happens to be away.
Perhaps a CPA or a gym teacher could then open it.
Perhaps one of the local colleges offers a class
        in opening 21st century mail.
Perhaps I should become a recluse.
Perhaps I already have.

STANDING TALL

I confess, I watch a lot of TV and I see a lot of commercials.
I don't know which is worse, the programs or the commercials.
Probably the commercials because at least the kids and other still
     developing minds enjoy the programs.
And that's worth something.
But the commercials, in particular the drug commercials,
     the "wonder" drug commercials of the 21st century, that's a
     different story.
     It's also a scary story,
     for the sole purpose of the drug commercial is to promote a
     cure-all for every conceivable human ailment:

- drugs for arthritis and rheumatism
- drugs for sinus and upper respiratory infections
- for heart burn and indigestion
- constipation and diarrhea
- for high blood pressure and high cholesterol
- drugs for bladder, acne, and wrinkles
- and on and on and on.

And that's wonderful.
What I don't appreciate, however, is how on the one hand a drug can
     offer a cure or relief for one ailment and at the very same
     time threaten you with a host of others.
What kind of deal is that?
I mean, who wants to swap ailments:

- high cholesterol for a disfunctioning kidney?
- depression for loss of memory?
- constipation for anal discharge?

But the one that stands by itself is the commercial that promises
     love, romance, and yes, virility.
Wow! What could be better, particularly at my age?
Unfortunately, this same wonder drug carries warnings of a variety
     of side effects:

- chest pains

It All Matters

- high blood pressure
- runny or stuffy nose
- cramps
- headache
- prostate problems

Not to be overlooked is the possibility of a four-hour erection.
Can you imagine "standing tall" for a period of four hours?
That's four continuous hours. That's 240 minutes.
That's enough time to have breakfast, go to work, and
          come home for lunch – or whatever.
On the other hand, four hours might not be all bad.
I mean, such a happening could surely stimulate the imagination.
At the least, you might get your picture in the paper or some specialty
          magazine.
And then there's always Ripley's Believe It or Not.
But all things considered, I think I'd be satisfied with the
          four-minute version.
I know my wife would concur.
Besides, what would I do with it for four hours?
Clotheslines are not permitted in my community.
Furthermore, do I hide it or flaunt it?
Hi, neighbor, look what I have!
Worst of all, what if no one notices?
I'd have to take another wonder drug for depression.
And then one for loss of memory.
And on – and on – and on.
So, I think I'll just pass.
I mean at my age who needs virility?
I'll just choose to remember; that's good enough.
And let's face it, today just remembering is an accomplishment.

Maybe someday when there are no side effects, maybe
          then I'll try the wonder drugs.
Until then, I'll just stay as I am, lovable and limp.
And, God willing, I'll remember how it used to be.

WHATEVER, WHENEVER

You need a plumber, perhaps an electrician,
      or a painter, carpenter, landscaper, CPA,
      – a service of some sort.
So you call the appropriate party for an appointment,
      and after leaving three or four unanswered messages,
      you finally get to talk to a living being.
What you hear goes something like this,
      "I'll be there sometime next week."
With a little patience and persistence you can usually
      arrive at a mutually satisfactory day.
Now comes the hard part –
      narrowing down the time to a.m. or p.m.
With a great deal of patience and persistence
      you can on occasion achieve this.
But that's the best you'll do –
      either a.m., sometime between 8:00 and 12:00,
         or p.m., sometime between 12:00 and 5:00.
To pin it down to an individual hour is wishful thinking.

Now understand, I left New York because I wanted to,
      because there was a lot I didn't like, or couldn't tolerate,
      or couldn't afford.
But allow me to say one positive thing
      about the "old" city. When you called for a service,
      you were able to set a specific time
      on a specific day and, best of all,
      the service provider usually arrived
      within minutes of the scheduled appointment.
You might well get "screwed" with the bill,
      but, like the job, it was on time.
Down here it's different.
      The price is right and the workmanship fine,
      but few care about time,
      and you could, if you're not accustomed to it,
      go mad from first arranging and then waiting for it all to

happen.

Recently, wife decided the house needed painting.
So she asked around, got some recommendations, and
      made some calls in an effort to get the job appraised.
It took better than a week to hear back from two different sources.
A third source never returned our call,
      and we never did understand the fourth source.

It was another week before we received estimates,
      one written and one verbal.
And another five weeks before the job could be scheduled.
One additional week for painting, and the job was done.
In case you're keeping track, our painting project
      took eight weeks from beginning to end.
The price was right, the workmanship fine,
      but we lost eight weeks of our lives,
      and at least a sliver of our sanity.

And then there was our tax preparation for the previous year.
We had been going to some local CPA
      for several years and felt comfortable with him.
So in February we set up an appointment for March.
We arrived early, more than fifteen minutes early.
Anyway, it took but a minute to realize that our
      friendly, comfortable-to-be-with CPA wasn't there,
      unless he worked in the dark.
Disregarding that possibility,
      we approached his secretary and confirmed
      our appointment.
Sensing that her life was in danger, secretary quickly made a few
      phone calls and "lo and behold,"
      after thirty minutes or so our man arrived, and
      with a drawl only natives could understand,
      he apologized for his tardiness,
      or at least I think that's what he did.
Only the promise of a healthy tax return
      stopped me from whistling "Yankee Doodle Dandy."

It All Matters

My lawn service guy fits nicely into this group.
He operates from a cell phone and is easy to reach.
The problem is that what he says doesn't mean anything.
In preparation for this year's contract,
    I requested a copy of the previous year's.
It took three weeks and ten phone calls before my guy
    with the mower admitted he couldn't find it.
I accepted that, as I couldn't find mine either.
So in an effort to start over, to achieve a new beginning,
    I requested a new written contract for the new year.
I'm still waiting.
It's two weeks now and I haven't heard back from him.
I just hope his tax return is made out by my CPA,
    and my CPA has his lawn maintained by my lawn service guy.
And, oh yes, I have just the painter for both of them.

This is indeed a different world with a different
    attitude towards work and time.
It's like, I'll be there when I get there,
    and if you're not there, we'll just do it another time
    – whatever – whenever.
Sometimes this philosophy can be a little difficult to accept,
    When, for example:
- Your house is on fire.
- The flood water's low spot is your living room
- The lawn is so high your wife gets lost
    making her way to the mailbox
- There's a glow coming from your TV set, but its not on.

Difficult or not, what is most amazing here,
    and what I'll never truly understand,
    is how most any inconvenience
    can become acceptable when treated with
    good ol' "Southern charm."
A few consoling, comforting words spoken in a
    honey-dripping drawl while accompanied by a
    gentile, gentle smile, and all anxiety fades away,
    and tomorrow becomes good enough.
    So relax.

It All Matters

Whatever it is, it'll get done, and if you're lucky,
      you'll still be around to enjoy it.
This philosophy is best described as
      – whatever – whenever.
Down here, it's a way of life and
      you either adjust to it or you go mad.
Right now, I'm sort of in the middle.
But then I've only been here 10 years,
      and I'm still adjusting.

It All Matters

RAGE

You could be anywhere and they'd be there, too.
It doesn't matter where or when, they'd be there.
Pick a place: a restaurant, rest room, movie theater, ball game, store,
    any means of transportation, and you will see a cell phone and
    someone of most any age operating it.
Take a walk in any shopping mall and what you see is people and cell
    phones and cell phones and people.
It's like the two have bonded and become one.
It's like how could you go shopping without a cell phone, or for that
    matter, how could you do anything or go anywhere without
    one?

I recently went to Quick Lube for a quick lube.
I figured that was the place to go.
There were four other people in the waiting room with me.
To my immediate left was a well dressed elderly lady, vintage
    grandmother.
As she was close by and speaking loudly, I couldn't help but overhear
    her conversation.
It was with her daughter, and they were talking about what mothers
    and daughters usually talk about – grandchildren and family.
Fortunately, after what seemed like forever, they ran out of names.
On my right, maybe three seats away, was a young man who was
    talking to his wife, or at least I hope it was his wife.
He was explaining to her where he was, how long he would be, and
    what his plans were for the day.
I got the feeling he was glad to be where he was.
Directly across from me, on the other side of the room, a couple
    shared one phone, passing it back and forth and talking to
    each other as they did.
Thankfully, I couldn't hear them.
I wasn't so thankful for the fourth person in the room who found
    refuge in both sleeping and snoring.
So there I was surrounded by three cell phones and one snorer, and all
    I wanted to do was read my golf magazine in peace and quiet.

It All Matters

There is another more serious aspect to the increasing use of the cell
     phone – when the driver of a moving vehicle
     attempts to incorporate his/her driving skills with his/her
     ability to communicate via the cell phone.
Not a good combination, as the driver's use of a cell phone is as much
     a distraction to him/her as reading or writing or self
     gratification would be.
It's not complex; a driver needs to focus on his/her driving.
Anything that distracts from that focus is detrimental to the
     effectiveness of his/her driving.
And if you want to debate that, consider how the combination of
     driving and cell phoning feeds man's latest dilemma, road rage.
I'm driving along watching the road, and I approach this car in the left
     passing lane going well below the speed limit.
I blink my lights to encourage the car to move over and allow me
     to pass on the left.
The driver ignores me, does nothing.
I gently tap my horn.
Again the driver does nothing.
I pass on the right, and there he is talking and laughing on his
     cell phone.
He's in a different world.
I'm in this world, and I'm furious.
I slow down, come abreast of him, and make a few rather
     explicit suggestions.
He "flips me the bird" and continues talking.
And he remains in the left lane causing a build up of cars behind him.
I think it must have been at this moment that I first truly understood
     road rage, what it feels like, and how dangerous it can be.
It also became quite clear to me where I wanted to relocate his
     cell phone.
Something, however, caused me to remember my age and
     the hopelessness of the situation. It was probably my wife. It
     was definitely my wife.
And so I drove on leaving behind both an inconsiderate fool and an
     explosive situation.

It All Matters

It was when the price of gasoline reached an all year high, and one
      looked for the best deal in town.
Satisfied with our find, wife and I waited in line with the other cars.
It was hot and the cars moved slowly.
Then the cars didn't move at all.
I looked ahead to the car at the pump.
Some guy in a business suit was standing there waving his charge card
      with one hand, and, oh yes, operating his cell phone with
      the other.
The pump remained in its holder.
Feeling my frustration, wife encouraged me to take it easy.
She went too far, however, when a few moments later she told me to
      relax, while this guy still talking on his cell phone and
      no gas being pumped.
Like a runaway cork, I popped and marched up to this
      jerk in a business suit.
In more of a growl than a voice, I suggested that he pump now
      and cell phone later.
He responded by calling me a bad word with the initials A. H.
Without hesitation, I returned the compliment, and the guy in the suit
      and I stood there staring at each other.
It must have been the foam in the corner of my mouth that caused
      him to pause, or perhaps it was my old age and the thought
      of his being brought up on assault charges.
At any rate, he pocketed his phone, called me that bad word again,
      and started pumping gas.

After a few sighs of relief, I returned to the safety of my car
      and the reprimands of my wife.
She was right; I could have been killed.

And if all this weren't enough, say hello to the new picture cell phone.
That's right. You can see the person you're calling.
Of course, understand that that same person can also see you, and
      that might not always work out for the best.
I mean, it's unlikely you're just sitting there, all dressed up, waiting
      for the phone to ring.

It All Matters

And so before answering, you first might want to tidy up a bit. You
  know, get out of your old bathrobe, run a brush through your
  unkempt hair, and apply a little much needed makeup.
In most cases, twenty to thirty minutes will do the job.
Of course by then the phone will have stopped ringing, and you will
  have missed the call.
But take heart – at least now you'll be ready for the next one.

Even newer and just as exciting is the video camera phone
  with Bluetooth.
I don't know what Bluetooth is either, and I don't want to know.
But the video camera phone will allow you to both talk to Aunt Betsie
  and at the same time take a picture of Fido leaving his
  "calling card" on your lawn.
How could you possibly do without one?
And can you imagine how much the driver will welcome it?
Now to take his mind off driving, he can both talk on his cell phone
  and take pictures with his new video camera.
In the slightly altered words of a great American adventurer,
  "That's one very small step for man and
  absolutely nothing for mankind."*

The question that remains unanswered and begs attention is how did
  my generation and all previous generations ever manage
  without the cell phone?
How did we ever run our businesses and manage our lives without the
  cell phone?
Could the answer be that we better organized our thoughts and days,
  we planned our trips, and sometimes we even thought before
  we acted?
And because of this now outdated approach, we didn't require
  "impulse" communication.
Considering that we managed without any kind of phone for
  centuries, and the Neanderthal's only means of communication
  was the club, and the Cro-Magnons couldn't speak English,
  considering that and more, is it not feasible that we could

---

* A revision of "That's one small step for man, one giant leap for mankind." Neil
Armstrong, July 20, 1969

manage very nicely today without the cell phone and other
related marvels of communication?

Well I can dream, can't I?

I can dream of a cell-phone-free society, can I not?

I can dream until reality sets in and I am compelled to realize that the
    nuisances will not be going anywhere, other than in more
    pockets.

And so the question then becomes, how do we cope with the cell
    phone, more importantly, how do we control it?

I'll tell you how. We enact and enforce two simple rules:

Rule One — Operating a cell phone shall be prohibited on
    any moving vehicle to include autos, buses,
    trucks, trains, trolleys, subways, airplanes, sleds,
    and all other moving means of transportation.

Such a rule would enhance both the safety and enjoyment of
    all travelers.

Rule Two — Operating a cell phone shall be prohibited
    within hearing distance of another human
    being.

Such a rule would support the right of privacy.

Together Rules One and Two would serve to preserve and
    protect the welfare of mankind.

Infractors shall lose all phone privileges for a predetermined period
    of time with one exception: a 1929 Bell rotary phone
    to be installed in, and operated from, the individual's personal
    residence only.

Isn't it amazing how an utterly complex problem can have an utterly
    simple solution? And all that is required is a fair, open,
    progressive, tolerant, imaginative, intelligent, judicious,
    vengeful mind – such as mine.

EPILOGUE

It is one year later.
My efforts to control the use of the cell phone have failed.
The "nuisance" has grown in both number and usage.
Now to add to megabytes and gigabytes, we have:
>   Micro SD cards, iPods, MP3s, USB cable, adnauseam.
Now Redtooth has joined Bluetooth, and it's just a matter of time
>   before another color is misused.
Now we have music phones allowing the operator to both make a
>   call and listen to music.
This "must have" introduction is priced anywhere from
> $150 to $500, the price determined primarily by the number
>   of songs that can be stocked in the unit.
That's a guess, as I neither understand how it works nor why anyone
>   would need or want one.
I mean, have we reached that point in our spoiling where we require a
>   phone and/or music to function?
I mean, what happened to thinking, when one would quietly
>   take the time to pay tribute to life and its experiences?
Where are we going with all of this?
Someone or something help us, please.

EPILOGUE'S EPILOGUE

I knew there would be more.
I just didn't realize how soon.
Now only months later the newest "tooth" offers:
>   the ability to send and receive E-mails, browse on the
>   internet, and maintain: a calendar, contact list, and journal.
I'd really like to go and hide somewhere, except I'm sure next months
>   feature will be a tracking device.

Beaten by a "tooth." Oh, the shame of it all!

IT'S MOO - MOO TIME

There exists today and for some time now a great need
    for an effective method of venting road rage.
Current methods of venting simply do not satisfy:
    counting to ten, turning the other cheek,
    smiling and wishing the offender a good day,
    counting your blessings,
    banging your head against the dashboard, whatever.
Nothing works. Rage dominates, and rage
    improperly channeled is dangerous.
The purpose of this writing is to introduce
    a relatively safe, yet entirely satisfying diffuser
    of road rage.

Let us first examine a few of the more popular causes
    of road rage, for in the cause we may well find the cure:

- making a turn or changing lanes without signaling
- entering a highway off a ramp,
  as though that guarantees right of way
- blocking the left passing lane by
  dallying well below the speed limit
- paying more attention to a cell phone conversation
  than one's driving responsibility
- attacking the road with a weaving series
  of "ins and outs"
- refusing to enter onto a road because
  there's a car somewhere in sight
- tailgating when the car in front is meeting
  or exceeding the speed limit while
  another lane is open for passing
- coming to a near full stop before turning off a
  major road
- going five miles an hour anywhere

Oh there's more.

It All Matters

The list is endless, but the results are the same:
      raised blood pressure, heart palpitations, voiced obscenities,
      twitching body parts, and a burning desire to get even,
      to stand up for one's driving rights,
      to advise and reprimand the violator of his or her infraction.
The need is clear. We need an effective way to release road rage,
      to defuse a temper that has gone out of control.
Most will agree that when the gnashing of teeth has subsided
      and an element of calm has been restored, all remaining rage
      should be expressed without inflicting bodily harm or
      vehicle damage.

Through years of research and countless hours
      of consultation with minds equivalent to mine,
      I have found such a way, a safe way to
      release this frustration, this pent up rage,
      a safe way to both inform and punish the offender.

Allow me to introduce, patent pending,
      my cure-all for road rage —
      the Derfla Moo-Moo gun.
Understand that naming the gun was more difficult
      than inventing it.
A very popular four-letter slang word would probably
      have been more appropriate than Moo-Moo,
      as this same four-letter word would have more accurately
      described the weapon's contents.
But, although found in the dictionary, this same word
      would have undoubtedly offended many,
      and so it was rejected.

So let's stick with Moo-Moo and understand
      that Moo-Moo represents that which is left behind
      by the entire animal kingdom.
Derfla, as a point of information, is the inventor's nickname,
      and is necessary for both patent and pride purposes.
It's also kinda cute and lends a warm, personal touch
      to the author.

Now that you have accepted the name as appropriate
        and as the best possible choice,
        imagine, if you would, the utter satisfaction
        derived, if when:
                driving along and someone cuts you off,
                or dallys in the left lane, or fails to signal,
                or speeds, or tailgates, you are able to fully vent
                by simply aiming the Moo-Moo gun and pulling the
                trigger.
Believe me, the violator will become well aware
        of his or her infraction and, best of all,
        your rage will have been fully and safely vented
        with damage done only to the violator's pride.
        Soap and water taking care of the rest.
Oh, the joy and justice of it all !
He or she, as sex is not an issue here,
        received what he or she deserved, and you saw to it,
        you made it happen
        with your new semi-automatic, air-cooled,
        lightweight Moo-Moo Gun.
I ask you, what other possible action could
        contribute as much to good, safe, careful driving?

Of course there will be complications:
(There always are with change.)
        •   initial shortages of ammo will encourage
            price gouging and an influx of faulty products.
        •   patent violations will need to be quickly exposed.
        •   the sale of convertible cars will decline drastically.
        •   an alarming growth of the animal population
            will occur as ammo demands escalate for quantity and
            color variation.
    and
        •   constant road cleanings will require a great new,
            expanded sanitation department.
    finally

- general unrest and mayhem will necessitate an expanded
and more efficient police department.

But as with all great inventions, the merits will
outweigh the problems,
and the Moo-Moo will survive and succeed
eventually rivaling electricity as man's
greatest invention.

And no bounds shall restrict its growth,
and the Moo Moo shall in time become
stantard equipment in all vehicles.
And the economy will flourish with the expansion of:

- faster, more maneuverable vehicles
- ammo factories offering a great variety of contents
- quick-stop repair gun shops
- one minute drive-in car washes
- miracle detergents

And animal farms of all kinds shall appear,
and all animals shall contribute to the great cause.
And collection agencies shall abound, and their business shall flourish
and prosper.

And Derfla will win fame and fortune.
And all will come to honor him.
And collection agencies will carry his name.
And the process of "subrogation" will become the process of
"derflagation."
And the world will be a better place.

Note: this article requires a good imagination, compassion for the
author, and probably a second reading.

PRINT ME

Somewhere along the line I started to enjoy writing, perhaps in
      college, perhaps in the sales marketing career that followed.
But it was not until retirement that enjoyment turned to passion, for
      with retirement came time, time to reflect on what had been,
      time to describe what is happening now.

The following tells of my efforts to get published. I mean anywhere in
      any form of print and with financial reward not a major issue.
Now understand, I would revel in any form of financial
      reimbursement, but honestly, my real goal was to see the
      results of my efforts in print – anywhere.
Family, friends, neighbors, even a few strangers all encouraged me to
      seek publication, and so I did.
Who was I to argue with fame and fortune, and besides, how difficult
      could it be?
You get a name and address, and you mail your work in – right?
Wrong, just about as wrong as you can be!
Getting published, meaning getting your work in print, makes writing
      child's play.
Put it this way: writing is always challenging and sometimes rewarding,
      but getting published is always frustrating and usually
      disappointing.
Put it yet another way: writing is fun, but getting published is a pain in
      that part of your body that gets out of a chair last.
And that's about as clear as I can make it.
Read on, and I'll tell you all about it.

After some serious thought, I selected three different types of
      publications for my work: a retirement magazine, a family
      magazine, and a local newspaper.
The names you don't need any more than I need a lawsuit.
It doesn't really matter anyway, since all three publications had one
      thing in common, a general indifference to the new and
      aspiring writer.
This became quite obvious upon scanning each publication for
      mailing information.

It All Matters

What I found, which was usually buried in the final pages of the
    publication was confusion: some names and titles, a few
    phone numbers, a few addresses, but nothing to indicate who
    to contact and how.
I opted for the editor as the "key," and that's who I pursued, calling
    whatever phone number seemed plausible.
What I got from all three publications was a recording thanking me
    for my interest and promising a return call ASAP.
What I did not get from any publication, for three days, was
    a return call.
On the fourth day with patience and good attitude gone, I called
    all three again and left what I promised myself would be a final
    message, first relating all that had transpired and then asking
    each if they were still in business.
Wouldn't you know it, that same day brought two return calls, two
    names, and two addresses.
Never heard from the third publisher.
At this point I was happy with two out of three.
It didn't take long for me to fill my mailbox with introductory letters
    and what I considered my best short stories.
At last I was in business, or so I thought.
Each day I would eagerly check the mail for a response.
Each day I would visualize an acceptance envelope, and each day I just
    knew that tomorrow would be better.
After three months of wishful thinking, I realized that tomorrow
    would only bring more of the same – nothing.
Amazing how a college education inspires reality!
Unable to figure out what was wrong, I did what came easiest, I
    continued to write.
As I said, writing is always challenging and sometimes rewarding, and
    oh yes, it also serves to take one's mind off everything else.

It was my always optimistic daughter-in-law who, hearing of my
    dilemma, found and forwarded to me several books that clearly
    explained the error of my ways, regular "how to's" for the
    aspiring writer, presenting in great detail a host of
    sure-fire tips on how to sell what you write.
It didn't take long to realize that one doesn't just send in a

"masterpiece," one sends in a "masterpiece" a certain way,
their way, whatever way they have established as the best way
to review and evaluate the multitude of daily entrees received.
And here I thought I was the only one waiting to be discovered!
Oh well, the books would explain it all – and in just hundreds
of pages.
And all I had to do was take the time out to read them.
Which I did, and it cost me seven days and seven migraines.
Let's just say the books had more do's and don'ts than I have words.

Perhaps we should start with the editor, for he/she was to me the
necessary target for all correspondence, the one who must be
reached and from whom support is essential, if one's words are
ever to be seen in print.
Below are listed a few of his/her personal "guidelines."
If you call them requests, you'd be closer to the truth.
If you call them demands, you'd be right on.
In no particular order, they are:

- Use only block type that is current and clear.[*]
Meaning I have to change my two-year-old
typewriter ribbon

- Double space your copy.
Sure, and keep everything on one page

- Proofread your copy for spelling and grammatical errors.
And here I was just going to guess at everything.

- Make sure your writing is clean and crisp.
Now "clean" I understand , but when I see "crisp," I see bacon,
and what does bacon have to do with writing?

- Leave 1½ inch margins on the left side, 1 inch on the top
right, and 1 inch on the bottom.
You gotta be kidding!

---

[*] McCollister, John *Writing for Dollars* Barnes & Noble, 1995

It All Matters

- Use paper clips. No staples.
How about contact cement?

- Never fold your material. Use a nine-by-eleven inch envelope
with a cardboard backing.
Because if it were folded, it would require opening,
and you know what a nuisance that can be.

- To identify your work, type your name, address, and phone
number in the upper left hand corner of the first page. On all
other pages, place your name in the upper left hand corner
with the page number just after it, or in the upper right hand
corner.
Please read a few times and then explain it to me.

- Use first class mail only.
And here I was going to use parcel post.

- Include a cover letter of no more than one or two lines.
Remember – "clean and crisp" – like bacon.

- Include in your mailing a self-addressed, stamped envelope or
post card.
How about a complimentary lunch and some show tickets?

- Be patient; allow up to six (6) months for a response.
Maybe they don't realize I'm a senior citizen.

- Don't expect an explanatory reply.
God forbid. That would be helpful.

So that's it. Follow these simple guidelines and you might, just
might, be on your way.
That is, if your title is not old and worn, and you have avoided
clichés, and most important of all, if you have initiated all
written correspondence with a QUERY LETTER.

Nearest I can make out, a query letter has nothing to do with
gender or sexual preference, but rather is like a sample of what
you want to submit, a "teaser" if you will.

The query should also serve as an introduction to and explanation
of your work, describing how your article fits the publication's
individual needs.*

Not surprising, the query has it's own set of "guidelines,"
emphasizing brevity, neatness, correctness, and would you
believe, "laser like" focus?

Here are a few of these guidelines:*

- The query should be compatible with the personality and style
of the author.

The style I understand, the personality I'm still looking for.

- The query should immediately grab the attention of the editor.

I can think of a few words that would do just that.

- It might begin with the first paragraph of your book, or it
might not.

How about springing with just a few other, "mights?"

- It should show the editor how your article fits the makeup of
the magazine.

So if the magazine is boring, simply send in a boring
article.

- It should include a list of other articles you have had
published.

As I said, "a general indifference to the new and aspiring
writer."

Should you find all this a tad confusing, realize you're not alone, as
I seriously thought of replacing writing with crocheting –
that is, until I realized that there was probably an equal number

---

* McCollister, John *Writing for Dollars Barnes & Noble, 1995*

of multi-hundred page "how to books" available on crocheting.

But let's say you've played the game, you've seen it through, you've sent in the query and done it their way.

Now all you have to do is wait for a response that requests the complete manuscript.

Should this happen, should you be so fortunate to receive that request and survive the shock of receiving it, then reread the "guidelines" and proceed.

On the other hand, should there be no response to your query, which, if you haven't already guessed, is probable, know that you still have several options:

Option #1   Consider hiring an agent, which sadly is even more difficult to arrange than getting an editor to read your manuscript.

Option #2   Be content with a fan club limited to family and loyal friends.

Option #3   Continue praying , and if you're daring, persistent, and retired, keep trying: write and rewrite, mail and re-mail, and yes, follow the books' advice.
Perseverance has realized more than a few dreams.

As for me, I'm a dreamer.

I'm also daring, persistent, and retired, and I just purchased fifty nine-by-eleven-inch envelopes – with backing.

So beware, all you editors: I'm here, I'm ready, and I'm not going away.

How better to close this quest for print than with a laser-like focus – PRINT ME.

WE GET TOO SOON OLD
***** ALSO STUPID

My companion was my dog, Shadow, who like myself was happy to
    have something to do, even though it was just running a
    few errands.

Our travel schedule included the vets for dog food, the pancake
    house for human food, the bank for food money, the deli for
    lunch food, and the liquor store for something to wash down
    the food. We are a food-oriented family.

The most important stop was the post office for mailing the 2005
    Federal Income Tax Return.

I placed the envelopes on the dashboard and Shadow's blanket on the
    seat next to me, and off we went.

First things first, and that meant the pancake house for "the most
    important meal of the day," advice I take full advantage of.

Then it was off to the vets for Shadow's special dietary food and a
    brief walk.

The bank was next, and Shadow was rewarded with a dog biscuit.

Finally, it was post office time and the day's main mission, mailing
    the tax returns.

To my delight there was no line, no wait, and I sauntered right up to
    the counter where I placed the envelopes for proper postage.

It was at this time that I noticed something was wrong: one of the
    envelopes was open and showed no mailing address.

A second look told me it was my copy of the federal return with all
    receipts and records enclosed.

It was the wrong envelope to be mailed.

So where was the right one, the original, the one to be mailed
    to the feds?

I could have sworn I had put it on the dashboard along with the
    state return.

Had I lost it? Had it fallen out of the car on one of our many stops?
    Did the dog's leash drag it out, or could I have just grabbed
    the wrong envelope when leaving?

It All Matters

Where was this most important refund-promising envelope?

I hastily searched the car.
Then I thoroughly searched the car.
I lifted the dog up to make sure she wasn't sitting on it.
I even checked the trunk. I don't know why, either.
At this point anything seemed possible.
Perhaps I left it home.
Perhaps I just grabbed the wrong envelope, and the right one
        was still at home.
Best to call my wife and have her look for it.
Understand, I'm not very good with a cell phone – fingers too large,
        so I am forever striking the wrong number.
And then there's the problem of using both the appropriate area code
        and the correct starting and closing procedure.
And how do you explain starting a call by pushing a red button?
To this old-fashioned guy, red means stop, and green means go.

So I push green and nothing happens.
Anyway, after three or four or maybe five failed attempts, I made
        the call, reached my wife, presented the problem and held on
        while she literally searched all the rooms of the house with
        emphasis on the bathroom where I spend a considerable
        amount of time..
She also searched the garage, the driveway, the lawn, and the garbage
        can.
        –No envelope!
My conclusion was that it fell out of the car on one of my stops.
        I mean, what else?
I know Shadow eats a lot, but a large, tasteless envelope?
No, it must have fallen out and was on the ground somewhere
        waiting to be picked up.

And so, I did what I had to do: I retraced my steps from the pancake
        house to the vets to the bank – Nothing!
I explained the situation at each stop to anyone who would listen
        and then headed back to the post office.
Just maybe I left it there, and maybe it was found, and maybe

I was losing my mind.

All seemed possible.

So back to the post office I went, only to find it was closed for lunch
with an iron gate assuring no entrance to the counter.

An attached sign read "closed 12:30 – 1:30." It was 12:35.

I was five minutes late.

Timing is everything!

I noticed a bell for service of some sort.

So I rang it. I heard voices inside, and I rang again.

I figured some compassionate soul would answer the bell.

I figured wrong – no one answered.

Banging on the door brought the same response – Nothing!

After leaving behind a few special words, I left, returned to my car
and checked in with my wife – Nothing! She found Nothing!

I remember screaming and my wife's voice quivering as she ended
the call.

Even Shadow looked scared.

Taking a deep breath, I decided I had to stay and check out this
one last possibility, but first I had to regain my self-control.

So I took Shadow for a five minute walk.

Fortunately, it was only for five minutes, as I had left the car open
and my wallet on the dash board.

After some more deep breaths, I turned my attention to Shadow,
who by now was pretending she didn't know me.

And then with forty-five minutes to kill, I decided to
browse in a nearby furniture store.

It was either that or an equally close gas station, and since I've never
really been into gas or the pumping thereof, I went for the
furniture store where the prices soon confirmed my age-long
belief that I really didn't need any furniture.

When I got back to the post office, the "Berlin Wall" was down with
five somber-faced individuals already in line.

It moved surprisingly fast, and to my relief the same "robot" was
there as before, so when I brought her up to date with my
tale of woe and the missing envelope, she sort of smiled.

It was the sort of smile one might extend to a fool.

174

It All Matters

Feeling fully qualified, I smiled back.
With that she turned and began thumbing through a pile of envelopes.
Suddenly, a real, full, warm, and genuine smile captured her face,
        as she showed me my missing envelope.
There it was; stamped, sealed, and ready for delivery.
I had mailed it after all.
If new friend had either combed her hair that day or applied
        some makeup, I would have kissed her then and there.
But she had not, and it was time to go home and explain things to
        my wife.
The deli and liquor store be damned. I would save that adventure
        for another day.

On the way home I noticed a white slip of paper on the dash board.
It peered out at me from beneath the recently purchased sheets
        of stamps. Inquisitively, I pulled it free.
It was a post office receipt dated that same day, listing both the
        stamps, and the postage for two envelops – one to the state,
        and one to the federal government.
I didn't know whether to laugh or cry. So I did both.
Senility is a terrible thing.

Shadow will eventually recover, my wife will eventually talk to me
        again, and I learned an invaluable lesson – henceforth, all my
        tax returns will be mailed via my mail box. It's just a short walk
        down the driveway, and I have every confidence that
        I will be able to get there and back without a problem.
Just to be sure, I'll take my cell phone along with me, the new one
        that starts with a green light and allows for adult-size fingers.
Progress is a wonderful thing, and the learning process never ends.

THE OPTIONS ARE LIMITLESS

It's always the same. It doesn't matter who the doctor is, or what
his/her line of expertise is, the experience is always the same.
After signing in, you look for the most comfortable, most
secluded chair available since there's little doubt you'll be there
awhile, and sick people are there, and you can't hold your
breath as long as you used to.

Besides, you never were much for sharing illness.

So you look around, you find a chair, and, after the other patients
have stopped staring at you, you make a move towards the pile
of magazines.

There seem to be hundreds, mostly all outdated and mostly all
intended for those of the feminine persuasion.

If you're lucky, you'll come across a magazine devoted to fishing and
hunting, or perhaps if it's your day, a Sports Illustrated, or even
a Golf Digest, but most probably your source of contentment
will be limited to the Ladies Home Journal, Cosmopolitan,
Elle, or Southern Living.

After thirty minutes or so of searching for anything sexually
stimulating, a not so sexually stimulating nurse beckons
you to come forward.

"The doctor will see you now," she lisps, and escorts you to a second
waiting room. This one is more personalized, because it's just
for you. That's because it's hardly bigger than a walk-in closet,
and two patients at the same time would make a crowd.

You strip to your shorts, as instructed and wonder if you should lie
down on the examining table. You're tired enough, and
it looks comfortable enough, but the last thing you saw on
a sheet of waxed paper was a slab of meat, and so you pass on
the idea.

Know that there is absolutely nothing to do in a doctor's
walk-in closet.

Had you given it any thought, you might have brought a magazine
with you, even a lady's magazine, but you didn't, and so your
only recourse is to examine the contents of the little side table
next to you.

It All Matters

Breaking in reveals tubes of lubricants and a pile of plastic gloves. Unable
to imagine their use, you try to recall why you
   are there and what it was your wife told you to ask the doctor.

Some fifteen (it could be also ten or twenty) minutes later the doctor,
   who has spent at least that long in his own cubical, enters your
   room in a twirling, swirling motion that brings back memories
   of Loretta Young.
He inquires as to your health, and before you can answer he begins
   his examination.
In what seems no longer than five minutes, he has checked out the
   previous weeks blood test, your present blood pressure, your
   heart rate, your lungs, and your weight.
Before you can find your wife's list of concerns, your doctor twirls
   his way out of your closet back into his cubical thus
   assuring the next patient will wait as long as you did.
Waiting in line to pay what Medicare will not and making the next
   appointment is next and (thank you, God) last.

All this became quite personal when back problems and my wife's
   insistence, mostly my wife's insistence, caused me to seek
   professional help. She said she couldn't stand my discomfort
   and pain any longer. When I questioned her as to whose
   discomfort she was referring to, she replied, "Ours."
   Unlike myself, my wife's a sharer.
So, I did what I had to: I made an appointment with a neurosurgeon.
The waiting room was larger than what I was accustomed to.
It was strangely empty upon my arrival. I mean empty. I mean, no one
   was there.
Perhaps, I thought, the patients got tired of waiting and left.
On the other hand, with no one ahead of me, it just might make for a
   quick call.
The nurse blew that theory, when she handed me a pile of medically
   related questionnaires. This involved filling out more forms
   than was required when I applied for college. A government
   application form would have seemed short by comparison.
After some twenty minutes of guessing at the answers, I returned the
   forms and continued my search for a man's magazine.
I was doing just that, when the nurse called me back to complete the

177

questionnaires. I had overlooked the back side of every
form – more questions more guesses, more time.

Again, I returned the forms to the nurse.

Again, I waited for the doctor.

Another fifteen minutes or so and I was escorted into their walk-in
closet with the usual framed diplomas, side table, and wax-
paper-covered examining table.

I never did check the side table for lubricants or gloves because the
thrill was gone.

Twenty minutes later, Herr Doktor made his appearance.

There was neither the twirling, swirling motion of Loretta nor the
warmth and congeniality of a Marcus Welby, MD. There was
only this arrogant little shit who could have cared less and
easily popularized a monocle.

Anyway, I lost both my cool and my mind, and I complained about
the more than one hour I had been waiting.

Herr Doktor kept both his cool and his mind and asked me if I would
prefer to come back another time.

"Perhaps another day would be better," he said.

"Perhaps now," I said and handed him my ten year old MRI, which
my wife had safeguarded all these years.

Herr Doktor glanced at the pictures and without the slightest
hesitation, or God forbid, compassion, advised me there was
nothing he could do since most all disks were in a state of
irreparable deterioration. "Degenerative disks," he said.

I said, "You mean my disks are kaput?

He replied, "Alles kaput." I took that for more than kaput and
grabbed my MRI pictures and headed for the door.

Although tempted, I neither slugged, nor saluted Herr Doktor.

Before I could make my escape, Herr Doktor caught up and directed
me to the hungry looking nurse with dollar signs for eyes.

On the way home I made a solemn commitment to begin each day
with a prolific series of stretching exercises. I still had the
instructional brochure the neurosurgeon had given me ten
years ago.

This way, I figured, I could stay home and leave the waiting and
paying to someone else.

It All Matters

And certainly as a college graduate I could make better use of my
time as in:

- counting the rain drops strike my neighbor's car
- taking a survey of the community's favorite vegetables
- finding a way to open the mail without damaging its contents
- learning how to precede a nap – with a nap
- finding a way to reach my toe nails
- brushing dog hairs off my clothing
- brushing dog hairs of my wife's clothing
- finding a new home for our dog

The options were limitless.

It All Matters

XMAS SHOPPING FOR AN ORANGUTAN

It should have been an easy day of Xmas shopping. It was only for
      one person, and it was basic stuff-shirts, a calculator, cologne,
      sox.

I mean, how easy is that?

Wife and I had completed most of our Xmas shopping early in
      November, and now all that remained were these few
      basic items.

We planned our attack, decided on the best departure time,
      selected the most appropriate stores, and agreed on the route
      to take.

And off we went.

Like, what's the big deal?

The big deal began when we got so involved in reviewing our plans
      for the holidays that we missed our turn off the expressway
      and had to circle back around through local traffic.

Our destination was a maze of stores, too large to call a shopping
      center and too small to call a country.

For a reason I can't explain, unless it was again the traffic, we also
      missed our turn into the maze.

In case you're counting, that makes 0 for 2 –
      2 necessary turns, 2 misses.

Making a "U" turn meant traveling through a residential area and
      eventually turning around in someone's driveway.

Our invasion of privacy went unnoticed, and I assumed the
      inhabitants were also out shopping and suffering along with us.

Fearing one of my dreaded temper tantrums was at hand, wife
      navigated us quickly back to the shopping maze, which as
      I recall, brought back memories of Disneyland.

As shirts were foremost on our list, we immediately sought out the
      largest, best known men's clothing store in the country.

By checking the skyline for store signs and neon lights, we sighted our
      goal, parked our car and, along with a few thousand other
      shoppers, charged into the store.

Surely the worst was behind us.

It All Matters

I mean, we were there, and all that remained was to find the
     shirt department and locate a button-down, size 17" X 36/37."
Frankly, I hadn't given the shirt size much thought.
I know my son had rather long arms, since I had on occasion seen
     him pick things up off the floor without bending.
But, so what?
This was a branch of the largest men's clothing store in the U. S.
It was immense. I calculated there was no way it would fit into a
     regulation size football field.
Surely, they would have every style and size of shirt.
After blindly moving forward some 40 yards, we got smart and asked
     for directions.
Another 40 yards, another series of first downs, and there it was, a
     literal shirt haven: piles and piles, colors and colors, styles
     and styles of more men's shirts than I had ever imagined.
Feeling the trip was worthwhile, we smugly began our search for a
     button-down, size 17" X 36/37."
Thirty minutes later we were still searching, and I was no longer smug
     nor was I returning each shirt to its original pile.
Realization came slowly, but it did come. Size 17" X 36/37" was not
     available in any style in any color in this store.
I flirted with the idea of giving my orangutanian son a short-sleeved
     shirt, but wife reminded me that he wore a long-sleeve shirt to
     work each day.
I, in turn, reminded her that his long-sleeved shirts barely covered
     his forearms.
Rather than pursue the discussion further, wife and I decided to leave
     and try another store, a branch of the second largest men's
     clothing store in the U. S.
As we searched for an exit, we noticed a team of employees rushing to
     restore order to their besieged shirt department.
I didn't know whether to cheer or cry, so I just waved goodbye,
     making sure it was a wave and not a one-finger salute.
It was, after all, the Holidays.

On getting to the maze, a lack of concentration had caused us to miss
     two turns.
Now, a failure to remember our point of entry left us at a loss as
     to where to exit.

And so we walked, following the perimeter of the store and searching
for what seemed like the appropriate exit.

It wasn't easy, as they all looked alike.

Finally, after probing the length of a football field, wife decided we
had at last found our point of entry. I wasn't so sure and
expressed my doubts.

Always a control-type gal, wife grabbed the car keys along with the
beeper and advanced to the parking lot, leaving me behind
to watch and learn as she beeped her way through the rows of
parked cars, her little white head bobbing up and down as
she went.

Just as I began to appreciate her initiative, she disappeared.

Suddenly there was no wife, no little white head bobbing up and
down, just a few slowly moving cars looking for a place
to park.

My first thought was that wife had been kidnapped.

My second thought was rational.

I mean, why would anyone kidnap my wife?

Surely, not for our car or money, and certainly not for a
shopping companion.

But even throwing out the possibility of a kidnapping,
I had to accept the fact that I was alone, without
transportation, and stranded in a hostile environment.

What to do?

To search for her would have meant leaving our last point of contact.

So I stayed, anxiously scanning the rows of cars for her little
white head.

As if to say I had suffered enough, she suddenly appeared driving
our car and beckoning me to join her.

"Wonder Women" had triumphantly returned.

She was as proud as I was annoyed, and we spent the next
fifteen minutes yelling at each other in the true Holiday spirit.

According to wife, I had no reason to be alarmed and should have
figured out that she had walked around the corner to search
the next parking lot.

After making sure she had the last word, she suggested we try another
store, also a "giant" in the men's clothing industry and also in
the same shopping maze.

Best of all, the store was offering a 50 percent discount on all shirts.

It All Matters

And so rather than strangle her, which was my initial intent, I yielded
and off we went.

Amazing what a positive effect a 50 percent discount can have on a
tormented soul.

No problem finding men's clothing store number 2; it also had a
skyline filled with blinking neon lights.

We probably could have seen it from the expressway, or for that
matter, the next county.

Anyway, before we knew it, we were there, in the shirt department,
searching once again for size 17" X 36/37."

Believing my actions to be out of the ordinary (I was tossing rejected
shirts up in the air) a saleslady came running over offering
her assistance.

When I informed her of our quest for a 17" X 36/37" button-down,
she proceeded to restack the disturbed piles of shirts while
at the same time suggesting we try the store up the street,
which she claimed was known for its unusual sizes.

I reeled from her insinuation – she was referring to my son.

Had I, with my perfectly proportioned body, sired an orangutan?

With injured pride and little else to lose, we headed for the store up
the street with the unusual sizes.

Upon entering, a saleslady loudly informed us that all modern Italian
shirts were on sale.

I replied, "Wonderful! How about the old-fashioned American
button-downs?"

She said the store carried only modern Italian.

After wife cast an Italian curse on her, which almost immediately
changed the saleslady's accent to Hungarian, we left.

Tired, dejected, and hungry, we agreed to combine our next stop with
lunch because in food, there would be strength and new resolve.

And so we drove out of the maze to a nearby shopping center.

It was there that I noticed a restaurant featuring bison burgers.

Feeling this might provide the turnaround we needed, we agreed
to give the bison his chance.

Let me just say that a bison burger is exactly what one needs to satisfy
a craving for something dry and tasteless.

It was so bad that I enjoyed the instant, overly sweetened ice tea that
   accompanied it, and before long found myself eager to
   continue the quest for the "orangutanian" shirt.

Fearing for my sanity, wife intervened and insisted we stop the search
   and provide my son (or his wife) with a check and request that
   they take over the shirt quest themselves, thus freeing us to
   seek out the other gifts: a basic calculator, an everyday cologne,
   and anyone's black sox.

And that's what we did.

For the calculator, we selected one of the largest electronic stores in
   the area. I mean, why break a bad habit?

We asked for directions and in a few minutes were ogling an entire
   section of calculators – all kinds addressing a host of varied
   subjects, all designed to save time and make life's little
   challenges easier: calculators for algebra, geometry,
   trigonometry, calculus and statistics: calculators for
   chemistry, physics, and biology, for business and finance.

One calculator served as a 50,000-word dictionary and a bookmark.
   Another multi-featured an address book, a calendar/planner,
   an English, Spanish, and French translator and a spell check.

It was all there, everything, that is, except for a basic, no-frills-attached
   calculator. You know, one whose function is limited to
   addition, subtraction, and multiplication.

That they didn't have.

Confirming the obvious inventory deficiency with a sales person,
   and expressing quite clearly, and probably too loudly, my utter
   astonishment at the store's failure to satisfy such a basic need,
   I grabbed my white-haired, now red-faced wife, and sought
   the nearest exit.

My fear was that she was going to cast another spell.

Suddenly, before ever reaching the exit door, we both started laughing,
   and the more we laughed, the louder it got.

After all the anxiety and disappointment the day had brought,
   the laughter felt good, and while I'm sure some shoppers were
   shocked at our behavior, their stares only served to fuel our
   new found release.

It All Matters

The Christmas spirit had descended upon us, bringing joy and putting
       everything in perspective.
We walked aimlessly though the mall, and for no reason other than
       the store before us now was smaller, less pretentious, and with
       no blinking neons, we entered.
It was here within minutes and with the help of a salesman that we
       found and bought a basic, no-frills attached calculator at a cost
       less than that of a bison burger.
We were on a roll – FA-LA-LA-LA-LA, LA-LA-LA-LA
I found myself whistling "Jingle Bells" and added a noticeable skip
       to my gait as we sought out the cologne.
Again, no problem – a few directions, and there it was, the right size
       with the desired spray apparatus at a reasonable price.
"Oh Come All Ye Faithful" replaced "Jingle Bells," and we headed
       home.

Once there, it didn't take me long to call my daughter-in-law, like
       about three minutes, and in full and dramatic detail describe to
       her our difficulty in locating a shirt for her unusually
       proportioned husband.
Before she could make a suggestion, I gave her mine.
I gave her the option of either accepting our check and finding
       the shirt herself or providing us with another gift suggestion,
       such as a bunch of bananas.
She's a good kid, and knowing me and realizing I was on the verge of
       disowning my son, she agreed to do the shopping for us.
       I didn't care for what; it was hers to decide and do.

Oh yeah, the black sox.
Not a problem – I gave son a couple of pairs of mine, highly
       stretchable and without holes.
"You do what you gotta do!"

On looking back, I realize our shopping venture could have been
       worse. We could have been searching for shoes for him.

Can you imagine trying to locate a size 14½ EEE?

I don't think so. Not this shopper, anyway.
No, next year would be different.
Next year would be all cash.
I would retreat to my desk, grab my checkbook, and in a few
      moments conclude my Christmas shopping.
"Joy to the World," indeed.

EPILOGUE

Just when you think you have it all worked out, something comes
      along to make you wish you hadn't bothered.
That very evening, upon checking the day's mail of two bills and
      eleven catalogues, we couldn't help but notice one catalogue
      in particular.
It was from a clothing catalogue outlet, one of the largest in the
      country.
So we looked, and in less time than it took to eat a bison burger,
      we found our orangutanian shirt.
There it was in all its glory: size 17" X 36/37," button down,
      in a variety of colors.
The fact that shipping and handling fees added considerably to the
      cost didn't matter; a small price to pay for one's sanity.
Oh yeah, we ordered.
We also informed our daughter-in-law of our miracle find, and
      concluded our longest day by singing every Christmas
      carol we could think of.

And regarding next year's shopping plans,
      I think we'll just wait and see.
Although, I have to tell you, the concept of buying personal gifts for
      everyone through a catalogue while leaving the car in the
      garage has a certain attraction to it, much like placing a magnet
      next to a BB.
It might even explain the tears of joy that bring a smile to this tired
shopper's face.

IT'S CHRISTMAS TIME AGAIN ---- FA-LA-LA-LA-LA, LA-LA-LA-LA

That means it's travel time.
And that means it's motel time.
And that means before long, you'll wish
    you had invited everyone to your house.

Too frequently your holiday trip goes something like this:
    You've had a long, tough day traveling
        in your gas-guzzling SUV.
    You've observed the countryside in great detail,
        thanks to hours of stop and go traffic.
    And now at long last you've arrived at your
        "home away from home."
    Armed with the magic key-card and using
        all the skill and the patience you can muster,
        you fiddle your way into the room.
    After checking out the TV to make sure it works
        and adjusting the A/C to make sure you can breathe,
        you realize you are tired and
        much in need of a refreshing shower.
    So you do what you're supposed to do.
    You remove your clothes and stand by the shower.
    You adjust the showerhead, turn the water on,
        and then watch as the water streams
        out of the tub facet into the tub.
Unfortunately, you don't want a bath.
You want a shower.
As there are no directions, you do the only thing you can do.
You play with the knobs, something you have always enjoyed doing.
You experiment – you push, pull, and before long you find yourself
    praying, all to no avail.

And so the question arises, should it require an engineer to determine

how to get the water to flow out of the shower head?
And know that all showers are different.
Don't think for a moment that if you've solved one, you've solved
    them all, because each motel has its unique showerhead-
    facet design.
And each one requires its own step-by-step procedure, all brilliantly
    conceived by someone who hates travelers.
But let's say you're lucky and get the shower to work, and water
    flows from the showerhead.
Now, all you need to figure out is how to get hot water.
What could be easier? Red for hot, blue for cold.
Unfortunately, either the colors have faded beyond recognition,
    or there is no visible indicator.
And so the only way to adjust the water temperature
    is to fiddle with the dials.
A little too much fiddling either way, and favorite youthful
    expressions come to mind.

But God is all-merciful, and so eventually you'll do it.
You'll figure it out.
You'll balance the hot and cold water, and you'll take your shower.
Life is good – FA-LA-LA-LA-LA,
            LA-LA-LA-LA!

There is an option, you know.
When you've been traveling and you're tired
    and need to be refreshed – take a bath.
Here, all you need to figure out is how to drain the tub.
And if that's a problem, just leave it.
Some engineer is sure to come along and drain it for you.

But let's move on, because your motel adventure continues.
Entirely apart from the challenge of the shower
    is the ever-lurking danger of the toilet flush.
Easy to initiate and requiring just a flick of the lever, the toilet flush
    may nevertheless give rise to a sucking action of dynamic,
    deadly proportions.
With that in mind, never, ever, under any circumstances,

It All Matters

bend over the toilet while flushing, lest you find yourself
on a cruise to a very different world.
And I don't mean the Caribbean.
Furthermore, under no circumstance
should you engage the lever while wearing anything around
your neck such as a neck tie, scarf, or necklace.
It is a fact that all have been directly attributed to the unexplained
disappearance of more than a few motel guests.

So, play it safe when your travels include a motel stop
and pack an ample supply of Kaopectate,
or, if that seems a little extreme, consider a Port-A-Toilet.
In all sincerity, if you're traveling this holiday season,
have a safe trip.
And if you're not traveling this holiday season,
consider yourself fortunate.
Either way, Merry Christmas
and a happy, healthy New Year.

TO DRIVE OR TO FLY, THAT IS THE QUESTION

Neither is perfect; both have some advantages, and both have enough
  disadvantages to have you forget the advantages.

Driving is OK if you have the time, if you have someone compatible
  to share the driving with, can tolerate the inevitable traffic
  jams, have a decent motel to go to and a decent slow-food
  place to dine, can adjust to a room that is either too hot
  or too cold, are mechanically inclined and successful in
  working the shower, can tolerate the absence of an exhaust fan
  in the bathroom, are able to appreciate the location of the
  toilet, which makes possible finding relief and brushing one's
  teeth at the same time, are not effected by unusual noises such as
  footsteps outside your door or the on-and-off crank
  of the A/C and the up-and-down whirl of a nearby elevator,
  and, finally, if you find the one-hundred dollar plus ever
  increasing room charges acceptable and can tolerate the recent
  addition to the free breakfast, an unforgettable rendition
  of sausage and eggs that will surely have you searching for the
  Rice Krispies – then and only then, considering all there is to
  consider, should you choose driving as the "way to go."

And so, on a recent trip back north, wife and I, unable to forget our
  last driving debacle, decided to give the airways a try.
We had tried flying before, and it did have its advantages.
By carefully selecting flight days, we managed to reduce our cost
  considerably, and I'm talking hundreds of dollars.
Of course, we had to be at the airport by 6:45 a.m., which required
  a 6:00 a.m. departure time, and a 5:00 a.m. get-out-of-bed time.
Now, my wife is an early riser, so for her it wasn't much of a change.
For me, it had the effect of not going to the bathroom for three days.
Anyway, a friend, a real good friend, was kind enough to drive us to
  the airport. He probably had to rise at 4:30 am, and that might
  explain why he hasn't had a kind word for me since.

190

Anyway, the flight north was pleasant and fast.
And before we could take a nap, we were landing and then waiting for
    our luggage.
Another hour or so in the limo, arranged for by our son, and we
    reached our destination.
Travel time door-to-door – eight hours; vastly better than the thirty-
    plus hours required driving.
Was this the answer? Was flying, "the only way to go?"

Unfortunately, we had to return, and to fairly compare one mode of
    travel with the other, one has to consider both the coming
    and the going.
Allow me to tell you about the return trip.
Allow me to share with you this most memorable tale of the airways.
The scheduled departure time of 5:40 in the evening and arrival time
    of 7:30 p.m. the same evening pleased me no end, since it
    allowed for dinner and drinks upon arrival, musts for this
    traveler.
We boarded at 5:20 p.m. right on schedule and awaited departure.
At 6:00 p.m. we were still sitting on the tarmac.
Every now and then, mostly then, we'd move a few feet.
At 6:15 p.m. almost an hour after boarding, the pilot informed the
    passengers that there would be a further delay, because there
    was, in his words, "a mile of outgoing aircraft ahead of us."
I went along with the joke, and along with other passengers, laughed
    at the pilot's great sense of humor, only to realize after another
    fifteen minutes of sitting on the tarmac, that the pilot had no
    sense of humor at all.
Not only that, he was probably a sadist.

The lady sitting to my right, feeling the extent of my girth, was kind
    enough to tilt the other way.
I say "tilt" because her girth was as large as mine, and so despite both
    our efforts we seemed to be sharing the same seat.
Wife just sat there with her face pressed against the window staring at
    the line of aircraft ahead of us.

First, I heard her moan, "Maybe we should have driven."
This was followed by, "We should have driven," and then finally, "Flying sucks."

Not least of the irritants was the imp.
She was seated in the next aisle with an elderly adult.
I would have heard her had she been seated in the terminal.
The longer she waited, the more and louder she yelled.
Her first audible words were, "Go faster."
Everyone laughed. Her next comment, coming a few moments later,
    turned laughter to fear as she said, " I wanna go home now,"
    with emphasis on "now."
These same words with the same emphasis were repeated at irregular
    intervals, so one never knew when or if she would stop.
Understand this was no human voice – shrill, yes, but more accurately
    descriptive, would be to liken it to the cry of a wild animal
    such as a hyena – in heat.
I became concerned about both my hearing and ability to control my
    emotions.
The pilot's next announcement probably both saved the imp's life
    and prevented a riot on the plane.
His words, "I can now see the end of the runway" compare
    dramatically to General Mac Arthur's, " I shall return."
We crept along now at a noticeably faster pace, and then with the roar
    of the engines, we took off with the imp yelling louder than
    ever, "Here we go! Here we go!"
Those passengers with still enough strength applauded.
We were airborne.

It was 7:00 p.m., one hour and twenty minutes behind schedule.
    Another announcement a few minutes later allowed for the
    empting of bladders, a bodily function previously prohibited
    during the one hour and twenty minutes we sat on the tarmac.

The voice from the front added that no lines to the bathroom would
    be permitted. I assumed the idea was to leap from one's seat as
    soon as the bathroom emptied and beat the next bladder

to the "john."
I saw an old guy try three times.
He never came close.
Then I didn't see him anymore.
Perhaps he found another way.
Every so often I could hear muffled cries from the tail of the plane
    because those furthest away had little chance of getting there
    in time.
I, on the other hand, was seated in the sixth row from the front and
    the "john" and therefore was in a good position to gain entry.
Unfortunately, lack of nourishment and struggling with the fat lady for
    a fair share of my seat left me too weak to compete, and
    I patiently waited until there would be little or no competition.
I had another even better reason for waiting; the large lady next to
    me had ordered and was eating a double portion of Italian
    Biscotti, and chocolate Toblerone.
She appeared to be the only happy one on the plane, and she was too
    big to disturb.
And so I sat there waiting for her to finish before
    requesting passage into the aisle.
She ate slowly, as if swallowing would cancel out her appreciation.
I figured anyone eating that slowly and carrying that much weight
    would have to be chewing every minute of everyday just to
    maintain weight.
Anyway, mustering all the courage I could, I asked for passage and she
    obliged, and with perfect timing I entered the smallest
    bathroom I had ever been in.
The only advantage I could surmise was that it would be impossible to
    fall down.
An enlarged prostate kept me there longer than I wanted.
Further delay came when I was unable to turn off the faucet.
I pushed, probed, and pulled everything in sight.
The water kept running.
I thought of yelling for help, and then as if by magic, or some force
    from above, the water stopped; the faucet was on an automatic
    timer.
Well, they could have at least put a sign up.
Happy that I hadn't yelled for help, I returned to my seat.
What greeted me was the imp yelling, "I gotta pee."

A feeling of utter gratefulness over-whelmed me as I realized I had
     avoided an ugly confrontation – I had been there, done that.

Seated immediately behind us were two uninteresting passengers.
They were also loud and made no effort to keep their conversation
     private.
It was all computer talk, and what, to an imaginative, creative mind
     such as mine, is more boring than that?
Regardless of what the one said, the other would reply "exactly."
Back and forth went the "exactlys"
Only the imp's outcry put things in perspective.

Truth is, had anyone proposed securing the imp to one wing and
     the "exactlys" to the other, it would have had my wholehearted
     support.
As we approached the end of our flight, the pilot, in an effort to save
     his life and explain the late arrival, labeled this day as one of
     the worst ever for traffic out of La Guardia.
I might have forgiven him had he either explained or even apologized
     for the imp and the "exactlys."
For his sake, I was grateful he had made the announcement from
     behind a secured door.
All things good and bad come to an end, and we finally arrived,
     landing with a bump and a run down the tarmac.
The pilot yelled, "Whoa, Nellie."
The imp yelled, "I gotta pee."
And I said my first "Hail Mary."
A perfect ending to a flight that might well have been arranged by
     Hertz or Avis.

It was 8:40 p.m.
The pilot had reduced the late arrival time to one hour and ten
     minutes.
Luggage came next.
We walked like "Born Agains" to an unmarked chute and waited,
     hoping we were at the right place.

It All Matters

The other passengers joined us and that regrettably included the
imp, who viewed the baggage area as an opportunity to
show off her running and sliding skills, each lap including
both, along with a terrifying last-second plunge under the
baggage chute.

I gave serious thought to tripping her, but as I started to lay my plans,
I noticed what had to be the guardian of the imp.

At first I thought it was her grandmother, but on one of her laps
around the area, the imp referred to the grandmother-
looking lady, as Mom.

The "God help me" look on Mom's face did it; I could do nothing.
I could only feel for that woman and appreciate the fact that
my exposure to the imp was coming to a close.

A few minutes later, ours and another one hundred or so bags came
down the chute.

As I pulled ours off (we had four of no less than fifty pounds
each) I felt the strain on my back. Then as I toted them to my
friend's awaiting car and lifted them into his trunk, I realized I
should have had my wife carry the bags. She handles pain far
better than I.

Understand, it wasn't the bags that assured my not playing golf for at
least a week, it was rather the tortuous half seats on the plane;
the same half seats passengers were confined to for one hour
and twenty minutes as the plane sat on the tarmac, the same
half seats that had essentially one position, a position that
forced the upper body forward and supported one's neck only
if one's parents were Neanderthals.

The auto trip home was blissfully peaceful.

Our now former friend had brought his wife along for company.

Not only were they not talking to us, they were not talking to
each other.

I got the definite feeling that any future flight plans would be without
their assistance.

When I casually indicated that our flight did not include refreshments
of substance, my former friend responded, "I'm not stopping!"

We arrived home at 10:00 p.m. thanked them, and waved goodbye.

And at last we entered our very own domain.

It was time for food and drink.

Wife was more interested in unpacking and getting settled.

So while making drinks, I decided on a food plan.

It was simple and straightforward: I would distribute all the bags to
the rooms of her choosing and unpack each bag. This did not
include putting the contents away, just emptying the bags.

Wife, in turn, would scramble up some eggs and thus prevent my
passing out from malnutrition.

She bought the deal, and as I distributed and unpacked the bags, I
could hear the beating of eggs.

Unfortunately, what little patience I had left deserted me, and I
proceeded to prod wife into completing her part of the deal.

I mean, how could I know she was also cooking up some ham
and biscuits?

Wife's reaction was unkind and entirely uncalled for – as she physically
threatened me with the frying pan and its contents.

What to do?

How could I win this one?

That was my dinner she was waving around.

There was only one way and I took it. I apologized for my impatience
and gave her a hug and a kiss, while at the same time rescuing
my ham and eggs.

As my father always said, "You gotta do what you gotta do."

I don't know what I enjoyed more, the ham and eggs or my
wife's kiss.

Let's just say the kiss, since I don't know how I could neutralize another
frying pan attack.

Another hug, another kiss, and the day was history, as was the trip.

The question remains, however, to drive or to fly?

To me the answer is obvious – neither. Best to stay home and send out
invitations.

However you do it and whatever you must offer as a lure, get others
to experience the absolute joy of "getting away."

Whatever the inconveniences, whatever the cost, stay home and leave
the driving or flying to them.

THE LONGEST DAY
------ AND NIGHT

It's not that it was a bad day: no one was injured, or arrested, or
      committed.
It's just that it was a day I could have done without.
I don't mean I want to forget it, since one can learn from any
      experience.
And that's as positive as I can get about this particular day.

We left home on time: sons Kevin, John, and father-in-law George.
The traffic wasn't bad, considering we were on Long Island's
      infamous Northern State Parkway with Belmont Raceway
      as our destination.
The problem was not the other cars.
John, with his new managerial job, his cell phone, and his zealous,
      thunderous voice, they were most of the initial problem.
The kid, now in his late forties, has to speak loudly.
It's like he believes that if he doesn't, no one will hear him.
Always been that way with John.
And his hearing is fine; we had it checked as a boy.
So you explain it.
We tried, we really did, wife and I.
     We talked to him.
     We begged him.
     We even tried whispering to him, hoping
     he would adopt the concept.
The kid will not chance it; he will be heard.
And so father-in-law George and I had no choice but to attempt
      to cope with some 30 continuous minutes of ear-piercing,
      business-related phone calls.
John was taking his new managerial position seriously.
When, after a while, I begged for mercy, he informed me that he was
      just working, that this was his job, his modus operendi.
I thought seriously of replying,
     "Well, why don't you stay at home and work? Wouldn't that be

easier and best for everyone, except your family?"

But then I realized, if he had done that, I would have missed out on
an invaluable lesson in cell phone management, and so I said
nothing more.

When John realized he was getting hoarse and repeating calls,
Kevin took over and attempted to make arrangements for his
upcoming Las Vegas trip.

No ordinary cell phone for Kevin, but rather a hands-free, voice-
activated cell phone.

Nothing but the best for Kevin.

It's always been that way.

That's why we call him, "Big Bucks."

Anyway, I could tell John felt outdone by big brother's hands free,
voice-activated cell phone.

I was indeed grateful that he didn't ask to use it,
which would have brought him and his voice from the
rear of the car to the front where I was.

When you're desperate, you gratefully accept any break that comes
your way.

We finally arrived at Belmont.

I felt like I had been on an extended business trip and renewed
my vow to hate cell phones forever.

Valet parking took care of the car.

Well, let's just say they took the car.

More about that later.

"Big Bucks" and John took care of parking, admission, and programs,
and then, at "Big Bucks" insistence, we proceeded to the
exclusive club house area.

Feeling that I should pay for something, I volunteered to pay the
$20 seating charge, although I really felt I was capable of
seating myself.

Anyway, we were there with enough pre-race time to order lunch.

Our waitress recommended the sirloin steak sandwich for $15.95,
a real New York bargain, and that's what the boys and
I ordered.

I mean, I wasn't about to sit there with a tuna salad sandwich and
watch them chow down on a sirloin steak.

It All Matters

George ordered a salad, a simple unpretentious salad, which
       George said was good.
No one said the steak sandwich was good.
       The meat was ¼ inch thick and shaped like a hamburger,
       which it may very well have been a few weeks ago.
       It was topped with limpy lettuce and uncooked onion nuggets,
       and was surrounded by a mayonnaise soaked roll.
It was all I could do to eat it.
For $15.95, you give it your best shot.
My only drink besides water, which surprisingly they didn't charge for,
       was a Bloody Mary.
George had iced tea, and the boys opted for a few beers.
I guess they enjoyed the few beers, because before we left the boys
       opted for a few buckets of beer.

But let's move on to the main reason we were there:
       to gamble, to win, to at least pay for dinner.
I enjoy handicapping and had made it my business the previous day
       to fetch and study a Racing Form.
I mean study. I mean combining hours of intense concentration
       with years of racing experience in determining the day's
       winners.
George, who had won "big" last time had a different approach,
       he always bet the #2 horse.
He would bet this horse across-the-board in amounts you wouldn't
       believe and won't learn from me.
It didn't matter if the horse limped, had a two hundred pound jockey,
       or had never finished a race before, George's bet was always
       on #2.
John and Kevin combined both approaches:
       George's #2 and my miscalculations, and then added
       something of their own that I never did figure out.
Anyway, we lost, all of us, four people, four different approaches,
       eight races, and not one worthwhile hit between us.
Now add to the frustration standing in line to bet surrounded by the
       inhabitants of at least one nursing home, and you have the
       makings of a never-wanting-to-gamble-again scenario.

Picture it: you're losing and you think this at last might be your race,

you're in line to bet and time is running out, and who is
    ahead of you but a dozen grandmothers and/or great-
    grandmothers.
And what are they doing? They're asking the clerk questions,
    such as: "What is a quinella?"
            "What do you mean, the horse was scratching?"
            "Can I bet less than $1?"
            "Will I lose if I bet all the horses?"
Finally, when I heard one of the ladies describing her grandchildren's
    adventures to the cashier, I couldn't handle it, and so when
    she finally finished and passed by me in line, I sarcastically
    commented, "No need to hurry."
She stopped, looked at me and said,
        "That's right, Sonny, hurrying only makes you tired."
 I should have gone home then.

Only the lunch bill was more exasperating.
When it came, John picked it up and asked for $50 from each.
Understand that both he and Kevin believe that when you're with
        family, you always split the bill evenly.
Doesn't matter what or how much you order, could be just water,
        you split the bill evenly.
That's the "family way."
And who am I to question family values?
Anyway, John forgot to add the tip, and so he asked for another
        $5 from each.
And then yet another $5 because John didn't have his calculator.
In short: one ¼ inch thick, funny-tasting steak (or whatever it was),
        one Bloody Mary, and a seating charge cost me $80.
Add my $70 worth of betting miscalculations, and you arrive at a
        total net loss for the day of $150.
Oh well, the Bloody Mary was decent, I did come close in a
        few races, I did refrain from knocking down any old
        ladies, and best of all we were going home where I just knew a
        few Martinis would compensate for a lot.
I always like to be positive.

By now, it was raining and the New York rush hour was beginning.
We hurried to the valet parking area where Kevin presented his ticket.

It All Matters

It didn't take long for delivery.

It took even less time for John to notice a difference in the car:
the decorative hood ornament was missing, gone, bye-bye.

All that remained was a hole in the hood where the ornament had
once proudly stood.

I asked Kevin if that was why he got valet parking.

To his credit, he didn't hit me, but he didn't answer me either.

He just stormed off in search of a security guard.

A long 15 minutes later, Kevin returned with someone resembling a
storm trooper: big man, large body, hard eyes, expressionless
face.

I was relieved to see that he wasn't wearing a monocle.

After a brief but intense interrogation, "Fritz" had Kevin fill out a
bunch of forms.

I stayed in the car with George where together we tried to find peace
and quiet.

John stayed outside with Kevin.

Once in a while, he would walk off to the side and use his cell phone.

Even with the window closed we could hear him.

At last Kevin was dismissed, and we were ready to go and join the
other five thousand cars on the Northern State Parkway.

I wondered if we were the only car without a decorative hood
ornament.

The traffic was ugly – stop and go the entire trip home.

I had forgotten how bad the traffic could be at this hour.

What should have taken 45 minutes took better than 2 hours.

What made it all the more painful was the return of the cell phone
because now it was time for John's follow-up calls.

I almost welcomed it when Kevin received a work-related call from
his wife, Pam.

He considered the call important enough to require his immediate
attention, so, for the next 20 minutes or so, he actively
pursued the problem's solution using, of course, his hands-
free, voice-activated cell phone.

As I see it, there are three things wrong with this latest marvel of
technology:

(1) the user has to speak slowly,

(2) the user has to speak loudly, and

(3) the user has to speak directly into a dashboard mounted mike.

Should the user fail to satisfy anyone of the three requirements, repetition is demanded.

Not happy news for the driver, whose responsibility it is to make driving his or her most important challenge.

And not happy news for the passengers who realistically are thinking of throwing out either the driver or the hands-free, voice-activated cell phone.

Thankfully, it eventually ended. All the calls ended, the cell phones were put away, and we had peace and quiet.

And, although no one would admit it, we also had regrets, I mean, who likes to gamble and lose, or have his car ravaged, or sit in traffic for 2½ hours listening to the cell phone conversations of others, or, for that matter, who likes to try to do his job and listen to the complaints of others?

A little secret: what kept me going, what saw me through all this, was the thought of a chilled Martini or two.

This pleasant thought would come to an abrupt halt with a sudden discussion of dinner plans.

It was to be Chinese. That came easily.

Kevin's plan was to pick it up on the way home, since we would come close to passing the agreed upon Chinese restaurant.

John's plan was to pick up his car at Kevin's and go directly home where he was committed to remodeling a bathroom.

As it was getting late, John was anxious to go directly home.

Now you have the problem; a tired, thirsty driver and a committed, anxious passenger.

George and I just sat there, mature enough to realize that somehow this, too, would end.

And it did.

Always the diplomat and in an effort to avoid a brotherly squabble on a day when it seemed likely, Kevin yielded and headed non-stop for home where he dropped off both John and George – John to get his car and George to take a painkiller.

George, my hero, had suffered all day with a painfully infected toe that

It All Matters

I am sure negatively affected his betting skills.

Anyway, I was determined to see this trip through to its conclusion
    and, therefore, accompanied Kevin back to the
    Chinese restaurant.

The thought of a very cold, double Martini had nothing to do with it.

My mistake was in assuming the restaurant was up the street.

Well it was, except the street turned right and then headed back in the
    direction from which we came.

Some 15 minutes later I added to my many miscalculations of the day
    and subtly asked Kevin, "Where the hell is this place?"

You're not going to believe this, but Kevin yelled at me.

All these years, and he never once had done so.

Now he yelled, "Al, for Christ's sake, stop it!"

Amazing how a little stress can alter a personality!

I said nothing, and when we arrived a few minutes later, I sulkingly
    accompanied him to the bar where I knew my vision of the
    day awaited me.

Amazing how just the thought of a Martini can help one deal with
    adversity!

Twenty minutes and a few Martinis and Johnny Reds later, our dinner
    arrived along with a tab for $140.

Add Kevin's tip and you have a tab for $170.

Now this might be considered a little extravagant until you realize that
    price means nothing to Kevin. You want it, you get it, and so
    he got it, a thought process he acquired from his
    father-in-law, George.

My philosophy is if you want something, drop some hints and wait;
    someone may give it to you.

Anyway, I offered to pay, slowly reaching for my credit card.

Kevin refused the offer, and I could feel the hurt and anger of the
    day dissipating.

When I offered him $50 to at least help with the bill, he again
    refused. Now all was forgiven, all was made right.

Smart kid; he bought me off!

My third Martini came after we arrived back home.

Dinner followed shortly thereafter, and I was ready for it.

What I wasn't ready for was the hot, tangy, spicy, peppery, pungent
    nature of the food, which everyone else seemed to welcome
    and enjoy.

Unfortunately, "hot stuff" of any kind leaves me with a mouth on fire
    and any combination of indigestion, heartburn and acid reflux.

Also possible are gas pains and what naturally follows that.

So I did the only thing I could do under the circumstances. I filled up
    on Chinese noodles.

Things only got worse for me when wife, distant the entire evening,
    suddenly suggested before everyone that I make the coffee.

For 36 years of marriage, wife has made the dinner coffee.

And so I could only interpret her request as a dig of some sort,
    regarding I knew not what.

Either that or she was attempting to show off her control over
    her husband.

"Make the coffee, Al!" — "Right, Elaine!!"

I mean what's that all about?

Did I miss something?

Did she prepare dinner?

Did she miss me so much she became resentful?

Whatever, I gave her one of my, you'll-pay-for-that looks and then
    challenged her remark openly.

She in turn gave me one of her you'll-pay-for-that-more looks, and I
    could but stew.

Then it was Jayne's turn to stir the pot.

Jayne is John's wife, my daughter-in-law, nicest gal in the world,
    do anything for you.

Unfortunately, Jayne has spent considerable time in outer space, and
    her comments, therefore, don't always make earthly sense.

For the life of me, I can't recall what she said, but I remember it began
    with Al and ended in confusion.

I recall replying, "Where is that coming from, Jayne?"

Jayne just continued to laugh.

By herself, I might add, for I wasn't the only one who was still trying
    to understand her remark.

Eventually, I did the only thing I could think of, I stewed, something

It All Matters

I was getting quite good at.

With our dinner over, it was party time. The celebration got
     serious, the voices and the laughter got louder, and the
     conversations made less and less sense.
All without me.
I have a self-imposed rule; never drink when you're either
     "pissed off," have hunger pangs, or a mouth on fire.
No, I wasn't about to party.

The final curtain fell when Pam, Kevin's wife, nicest gal in the world,
     do anything for you, suggested the group play, Gestures.
Actually it was a little more than a suggestion.
I mean she didn't exactly say that we will play, but on the other hand,
     before anyone knew it, we were playing.
In case you're grown up and have never played the game, allow me to
     explain. Each unfortunate participant receives the opportunity
     to act out a word written on a card.
What makes this absolutely exciting and ever so challenging is that the
     participant has 30 seconds in which to accomplish his or her
     mission.
Failure means watching others make asses of themselves.
Anyway, Kevin went first and then George.
Kevin acted out a chair and George a flower.
I was embarrassed for both of them.
It all ended for me, the day, the evening, the family get together, when
     Pam placed the game in front of me and explained it was my
     turn.
I hope in time she'll forget and forgive the look I gave her as well as
     my departing words, "I don't think so; it's all too deep for me.
     Besides, I have some crayoning to do."
With that I bid the group a general good night and hastily retreated to my
room, where I plugged my ears with wax, wrapped a pillow around my
head, and cried myself to sleep.

Tomorrow will be better.
     Please God, make it better.

EPILOGUE

Some thirty days have now passed since the Belmont adventure.
Wife has returned to making dinner coffee.
I've recovered from the Belmont losses, and things have slowly
        returned to normal, or what I consider normal.
I am also happy to report that a new movement has started here
        barring the use of cell phones within hearing range of others.
It has gained considerable support and is growing in strength
        each day.
There is also underway plans for protest marches and letters to
        representative congressmen.
It all makes me feel good, and if they throw in a ban on children's
        games for adults, I'll feel even better.

Now here's what I can't figure out: I'd do it all over again in a
        heart beat. I mean Belmont, and family, and all the rest.
Understand, by then cell phone usage will be severely restricted, and,
        should daughter-in-law Pam, nicest gal in the world, do
        anything for you, suggest a children's game for adults, I would
        just feign fatigue or even illness, perhaps a headache such as
        wife frequently uses under different circumstances, and politely
        retire for the evening.
Anyway, I'm ready for Belmont: have racing form, will travel.
So where are the invites?

COMMENTS NEVER MADE AT A 50TH REUNION

"Well, I'm seventy-two years old, and I can honestly tell you I have a
    fuller, healthier head of hair now than I had when I was
    seventeen" * – diminished vision making that possible.
More news: "Wife and I recently took out a reverse mortgage.
It's great not to have to worry each month how to pay a certain bill."*
It would be even greater if I could keep my wife away from the
    shopping malls. She's popular enough and spends enough to
    run for political office.

Seriously, I have some really good news:
    all six of our kids are out of high school.
        And there's more – they're all out of the house, meaning
        Elaine doesn't have to share me with anyone.
        You can't imagine her "tears of joy."
And now when the kids visit, we require an appointment, and if they
    bring their kids along, we require an appointment and a
    deposit. It's called self-preservation.
Still more good news: "I just saved a bunch of money on our auto
    insurance by switching carriers." *
Unfortunately, we had to sell our car. We couldn't afford the gas.
Not to worry, I got Elaine a Schwinn.
I convinced her it was good on gas.

On a more serious note, Elaine and I are enjoying our retirement in
    Calabash, North Carolina, where we have spent the last eight
    years trying to classify a redneck.
Here's what we came up with:
    a redneck is an individual with a red neck, male or female,
    and sometimes it's hard to tell the difference, who lives in a
    pickup truck along with a shot gun, a dog, and a supply of
    grits, which can either be eaten or used as a detergent.

---

*TV commercial

Our greatest challenge was finding a way to communicate.
We couldn't understand them, so we asked them to write
 everything down.
Once I asked a redneck a question, handed him a pencil,
 and then watched as he picked his teeth with it.
That's when we resorted to sign language, relying mostly on
 head nods.
After a few months, they followed right along.

That's about all the good news. I mean, we've only been here
 eight years.
I'd like to close now with a meaningful quotation.
It came from I know not where or when, but I'll never forget it:
 "Happiness is a by-product of vibrant living, brought on
 by an inner productiveness." As I said, I'll never forget it.
I'll never understand it either.
What I do understand is that I'm happy to be here with you
 celebrating this, our 50th reunion.

 May the voyage continue.
 May the parade never end.

EPILOGUE

Lack of effort and poor timing on my behalf, combined with too
many boring speeches by others, prevented delivery of this one.
Planning is everything.

PART IV

OH, MY GOD!

Something about a mustard seed.

When lost becomes found.

When you let Him in.

SAYING "I LOVE YOU"

She walked over to me and I knew right away she was special.
I liked the way she walked, and I liked the gleam in her eyes;
       those big beautiful brown eyes that changed
       colors in a certain light.
She was very friendly, and we took to each other immediately.
In fact, I took her home that night, and we've loved each other ever
       since.
She's great to the touch and loves to be stroked.
She's content doing most everything, or nothing at all.
She's quiet and listens and obeys most all reasonable commands.
And she's forgiving and understanding and ever so patient.
And she doesn't drool.
She's my big, beautiful husky, Shadow.
For years now, she has brought me a special kind of happiness.

She's my traveling companion.
Sitting next to me in the car, she watches the road and listens
       to every silly thing I have to say.
When she's had enough and wants to explore, she'll paw me
       ever so gently, and I'll know it's time to walk her.
At home she's my shadow, always following me, always nearby,
       always wanting affection, which I freely give her.
It's easy to do and comes so naturally.
I don't even have to think about it.
It just happens.
I feel love, and I express it.

In the quiet moments of the day or night, I find myself asking:
       why is this expression of love so foreign to me,
       why is saying, "I love you," so difficult when love is felt so
       deeply, and why did it take me 70-plus years and a dog
       to ask these questions?
I mean, if I can freely and openly express love to a dog,
       why not to members of my family, my children, my wife,
       my dear friends?
Why is it so difficult for me to show love,

It All Matters

or simply say, "I love you," to people I love?
Does the answer lie in my childhood?
Could the explanation be that simple?
My parents came to this country shortly after World War I.
They worked hard and saved and provided.
My brother and I received more than most.
We lived well; we traveled, vacationed, and both my brother
    and I attended college.
My mother showed interest in everything I did.
She reprimanded me when I deserved it,
    and praised me for my accomplishments.
She was a stay-at-home Mom in the old European tradition,
    tending the home and raising the children.
My father was the bread-winner and devoted himself to that end.
He also had a great lust for life and enjoyed himself as much as and
    whenever he could, relying on Mom to raise the kids
    and make the home.
Mom was not overly affectionate.
She never embarrassed me with hugs and kisses, but I nevertheless
    felt loved through her actions and constant attention.
It was different with my father.
There was this space between us, a sort of stand-offishness,
    which I was to interpret as indifference.
For this reason, I was closer to my mother than my father.

I believe that in an effort to close the distance between us and gain
    my father's approval, his affection, his love I worked very hard
    at whatever I attempted and managed to do well in both
    academics and sports.
My reward was most always money and a few words surrounding
    "good" that I'm sure originated from my mother.
And as much as the money was welcomed, there was always
    something missing.
Throughout my entire youth, I do not recall one time when my father
    put his arms around me and said I love you, not one time
    when this little boy, or for that matter teenager, was hugged by
    his father and made to feel loved, truly loved, love that reaches
    out and brings hearts together.
So now I better understand myself and my reluctance to openly

express my innermost feelings. I was raised that way.

Now I look at a picture of my father's family, and I see another little
     boy, my father, along with his mother, seven grownup sisters,
     and three teenage brothers.
My father, the youngest and last of eleven children, sits next to a
     framed picture on a table.
It is a picture of his father, his late father, who would not be there
     for him as he grew up to love him and show him how to
     express his love for others.
Now I better understand my father – he was raised that way.

It is time to move on with my life and even try to catch up.
And while I hope I have conveyed feelings of love for my children
     through action and deed, rarely, if at all, have I expressed that
     love openly.
I do that now without reservation.
I love you my children.
I love you for who you are and how you have faced life's challenges
     and enjoyed its rewards.
I love you all as my own.
May your lives be as full and rewarding as you have made mine.

We are all to some great extent the outgrowth of our childhood
     and the parental care we received.
Oh, other factors play a part in determining who we have become:
     our personalities, other people, economics, environment,
     to name a few.
But they all fall short in importance to the understanding and
     love only a parent can give.
So grab your loved ones and give them a hug and tell them
     you love them.
Do it now, and all your tomorrows,
     and your life and theirs
     will be all the better for it.
Thanks, Shadow.

ABOUT THE WOMAN OF MY LIFE
09-17-2004

I first met Elaine at a Parents Without Partners dinner
some 36 years ago.
She sat at a table with little to say.
Her eyes were bright and she smiled a certain way.
She spoke of her children with pride and praise.
We were two lonely people with 6 kids to raise.
Well the two families merged and became one.
The challenge began,
The loneliness done.
And you know there isn't a day that goes by
that I don't "count my lucky stars,"
that I don't thank God for my Elaine.
And there isn't a day goes by
that I don't pray for her good health,
for she is after all my greatest wealth.
This is one fine gal, mother, and friend
and surely the best God can send.

Love to you, Elaine,
now and always,

Al

"Love lifted me, Love lifted even me,
When nothing else could help,
Love lifted me."

LEVAS 198

213

TWO FOR SCOTCH

As a retiree there's much to do.
Waking up each morning, that's a start.
There's also the first cup of coffee
and the morning's first fart.
Later, there's checking the mail and finding more bills,
and sorting the catalogues with all its frills.
Perhaps a shopping spree is planned,
or a golf game's at hand.
There's visiting with friends and dining out
and wondering what the new kitchen's all about.
There's watching TV and falling asleep
and renting a video and falling asleep.
But the highlight of each day,
the "heart and soul" of each day,
the hours of bliss never to miss
are those hours of fun with your special one.

So picture you upon my knee,
A scotch for you, a scotch for me.
Two for booze and booze for two,
And I love "youse" and you love me,
And oh, how happy we can be.
A scotch for you, a scotch for me,
The joy, the peace, the serenity. *

*Revised words of Irving Caesar
"Tea For Two" – 1924

A BIRTHDAY WISH FOR A 50 YEAR-OLD SON

February 20, 2004

Dear Kevin,

Let's go back some 37 years.
That's when I first met you.
Actually I didn't meet you then, Kevin.
I met John, Brian, and Terese, your brothers and sister.
You wouldn't come out of the bathroom.

It was later, a few weeks later, that I did meet you.
This time you were coming out of the bathroom.
> Over the years, I would come to learn that Kevin spends a lot of
> time in the bathroom, usually a good portion of every morning,
> afternoon, and evening.
No one knows what he does in there.
Nor is anyone willing to find out.
Anyway, on this particular day, he emerged from his favorite room
> and immediately challenged me to a sparring match.
I remember, I showed him my left hook, and then I remember he
> helped me up off the floor.
That's really not true, but I thought the story would serve to cheer
> him up. And at this crucial time in his life Kevin needs all the
> positive input he can get.
I mean, 50's a big year.
It doesn't mean you're "old," but on the other hand it does mean
> you've been around for half a century, and that's not exactly
> an overnight trip.
But you're not "old," Kevin.
You're getting there, but you're not old.
Old is when someone in a wheelchair offers you their seat
> – that's old.

It All Matters

Old is when you can't remember sex — that's old.
Besides, old is just a word.
Or, as your father in-law, George would say, "It's all relative," and,
      "You're only as old as you feel."
And how do you feel, Kevin? — Sorry to hear that!
Ah, Kevin, you're still a puppy.
On the other hand, if that's true, in dog years, at the accepted ratio of
      7 to 1, you are 350 years old.
Some puppy!

George isn't old either.
George is Corinthian.
Allow me to explain:
There are three stages of old — getting there, old, and
      Corinthian.
You, Kevin, are getting there, I'm old, and George is Corinthian.
Webster defines Corinthian as:

- gracefully elaborate
- loving elegant and luxurious living
- a wealthy man about town

That's George now, and Kevin, that's you tomorrow.
The word on the street from Broadway to the upper East Side is
      that you are the New Corinthian.

And that's good.
So follow George, take his path.
Stay young at heart.
Enjoy it all.
Love life.
And treat each day as though it were special, because each day is
      special.
Each day is God's gift to you.

Happy Birthday, Kevin,
Love,
Al

IT'S A SHAME

With regard to the happy foursome, it would appear that the best had
        already come and gone.
Settled in the same retirement community, a parting of the ways would
        tear the group apart.
The differences were basically between the gals, but as the guys have
        to live with the gals, it became a guy thing, too. I mean,
        "You gotta do what you gotta do," right, Alan?
And although living little more than a pine cone's throw away from
        each other, friends of four decades became strangers.
To this day, some eight years after retiring in the same community, the
        situation remains unchanged.
Forty years of friendship lost in a maze of hurt feelings and damaged
        pride.
It's a shame. More than that, it's a damn shame.
It's also unfortunate, wasteful, immature, inexcusable, inconsiderate,
        narrow-minded, and utterly avoidable.
Describe it as you will, explain it how you will, it shouldn't be, but it is.

And surely the situation isn't likely to change unless all parties come to
        accept each other as they are now, as opposed to how they
        were then.
People change, and you either accept that change and adjust to it,
        or you move on.
To preserve a forty-year relationship, I for one vote for acceptance
        and adjustment.
But then, I'm sentimental and remember the good times and the good
        things others have done.
What better way to initiate the healing process than to limit one's
        memory to the positive?
The latter remarks serve as indisputable proof that people do change.

Somewhere along the line (it had to be in church) I heard the words,
        "You shall love your neighbor as yourself."
Now, I think it safe to say that in some cases that might be
        difficult to do, since realistically just tolerating some

neighbors might be considered an accomplishment.
The point is: if it is right and proper to love a neighbor, any neighbor,
as yourself, than certainly it should be right and proper to
extend that same graciousness to friends, even more certainly,
to friends of forty years.

So, here's to religion and doing the right and proper thing:
to forgiving and understanding, to remembering the good,
to beginning anew.

BY HIS SIDE

My wife and I had been going to the same church on and off for a few
        years, mostly off.
And while we appreciated the religious ambiance that the church
        offered and welcomed the idea of going to church, there was
        something missing, like a thought that gained our attention and
        left an impression, a message to carry away and hold on to, in
        short, a sermon we could both understand and relate to.
For us, the sermon was the most important part of the service.
It was the deciding factor in determining whether we went to church
        or not.

Friends of ours, who were members of yet another church, spoke
        highly of their Sunday sermons and both invited and
        challenged us to come and listen just once, as that, they said,
        was all it would take.
Some weeks later, we yielded and accepted the invitation and joined
        them and, as they claimed, "that was all it would take."
It was what we had missed – a sermon of meaning, a sermon that
        both explained the scriptures and related its meaning to the
        present day, words and thoughts to reflect on, to remember.
No longer was remaining conscious during the sermon the greatest
        challenge of the service.
No longer did I need to fear the jarring probe of my wife's elbow.
I could hear and concentrate on the spoken word.
I could understand and appreciate.
Remarkably, Father Merchant sermons are delivered without a note.
He stands before his parishioners addressing the group as if they
        were one.
His mind and body pop with energy, and he uses both to
        communicate.
The message is clear; something to carry away and hold on to.
Hallelujah!

It takes a special person to give a special sermon.
Father Merchant, or more appropriately, The Rev. Dr. Wilmot T.
        Merchant II, the presiding rector of St. Stephen's Episcopal

Church in North Myrtle Beach, SC, is just that.

I look at him and shake my head in wonder.

He is truly special; someone to look up to, and I should add, listen to.

Father Merchant was ordained as a priest in Liberia in 1987.

Then it was off to the United States where he attended graduate
school in Massachusetts.

His first congregation was in the Bronx, NY, where he was
priest-in-charge.

In 1999 he joined his family in South Carolina where he served at
St. Stephen's Episcopal Church, first as education director
and then assistant priest.

When the presiding rector retired and other considerations failed
to materialize, Father Merchant was appointed interim priest-
in-charge.

A few months later, and with the recommendation and support of his
congregation, he was elected rector of the church.

The year was 2002.

He has presided there ever since.

Father Merchant is a big man both spiritually and physically. He is tall
and broad and appears strong enough to play tackle for the
New York Giants.

He has a wonderful smile, full and warm, and a healthy, infectious
laugh.

Best of all, he does not hesitate to use either at any given time, and
that would include during the sermon when he is apt to
sidetrack a serious thought with a humorous one.

"Never mind that," a favorite of his, will touch off laughter –
first his and then everyone else's.

We, my wife and I, and what seems to be all of the congregation find
this change of pace, this unexpected touch of humor,
a welcome respite from the seriousness and complexities
of the scriptures.

And his sense of humor is always at hand.

I say that because I have tested it on several occasions:

- Once, when passing through the reception line, and aware of the
Father's NY exposure, I greeted him with a typical N Y

expression. I said, "How ya doin'?" Without hesitation, and with a
serious face he replied, "How <u>you</u> doin'?" I followed
the script and closed with "Ya don't wanna know."
Right then and there, with a long line of parishioners
anxiously waiting to greet him, he took the time to do what
he does so effortlessly, so naturally, he laughed a long, happy
man's laugh.

- And then there was the time during confirmation studies when
  Father asked everyone in the class to present a brief personal
  history to include previous religious affiliation.
  When it came to my turn, with as serious a face as I could
  muster, I told him that I was a follower of Islam.
  The Father first appeared stunned, and then I imagine,
  realizing who made the comment, placed his head on the table
  and laughed so hard I became concerned.

That's Father Merchant!

A big man should have a "big" voice, and Father Merchant has just
that. It is strong and powerful, fitting his physical image
perfectly, and whenever he sings, his voice fills the church
and very probably, the adjacent church.
There is no doubt as to its source – it is Father Merchant, the big man
with the big smile, the warm heart, and God by his side.

Now I sit in the pew and stare at the large golden cross behind
the altar.
I think of its meaning and feel a tremor run its course.
My vision becomes clouded.
I bow my head and give thanks.
I am at peace with myself.

A CERTAIN FEELING

They all look happy, and it seems real.
It's always that way when I go to my church.
People I do not know greet me with a smile and a happy
       face and say, "good morning," like they mean it.
Of course, I return their greeting and even return a smile, but the
       difference bothers me; theirs is real, they are truly happy.
I do not understand their joy.
It is almost embarrassing. It is embarrassing.
What am I missing here?

And then there's "peace," the word parishioners extend to each other
       at a specific time during every service at St. Stephen's.
They rise, spin, and with a happy face, wish all within their reach,
       "peace". Again, I do not understand. A wish for world peace is
       a lovely thought, yet it is no more than that – a thought, a
       wish, a dream.
Then, weeks later at another service, a happy face greeted me with,
       "Peace be with you."
Amazing what a few additional words can do. Now I understood: the
       wish for peace is for the individual, for peace of mind, for
       inner happiness, born from a feeling of inner comfort and
       strength, a feeling growing from a connection to things
       beautiful, from love and giving of oneself and doing for others,
       from living with dignity and believing in Him. A belief that
       cannot be rationalized, analyzed, or explained.
A feeling that is, indeed, faith.
"Peace be with you."
What could be better than that?
What a wonderful, meaningful wish for one to both give and receive.
       Surely enough to bring a happy face to anyone, even me.

REGRET AND HOPE

There is always regret, something you wish you had done or not done,
    or done differently.

I have my share. This one deals with our children.

It is our failure, my failure and my wife's failure, to provide them, our
    children, with a religious background, seeds if you will, that
    could grow and ripen with age into belief and from that belief
    inner strength.

We were always too busy:

- too busy trying to get ahead,
- too busy finishing up one week and preparing for the next,
- too busy making a home and maintaining a house,
- too busy trying to merge two families into one,
- too busy squeezing some fun into the weekends,
- too busy to give our kids the most important gift of all, a gift given to us by our parents: a religious background, an introduction to God, a basis for believing in Him.

At the time, I thought little of it, since we struggled just to get through
    the week.

Today, I think a great deal about it.

Today, I wish we had found the time, perhaps made the time would
    be more appropriate, to sow the seeds of religion by making
    church on Sunday a family affair.

Surely, it could have been done.

Just as surely, it should have been done.

I look at our kids now, our middle-age kids, and realize they live
    without Him.

When I raise the subject of God and the importance of believing in
    Him, a glaze of indifference captures their stare.

Usually there is no comment, just a meaningless shrug of the
    shoulders, or on occasion, a condescending, "yes." And once
    in awhile, I'll get a "I'm not into that stuff."

Their response hurts.

Yet, I understand, for how else could they respond when no seeds of religion were ever planted?

Most troubling is that I know not how to open their hearts and minds
to Him.

I am aware that times change and that in recent decades in particular
mothers have taken on additional responsibilities to bring
in additional income and satisfy once put-aside ambitions.

There is, however, a price to be paid for this additional income
and self-satisfaction. The price is time: free time, family time,
God's time.

Too many of us target "all that money can buy" as our goal and lose
sight of all that He can provide.

In so doing, we short-change our children; we replace inner strength
with superficial pleasures.

In this regard, I failed my children and find myself now turning to
should, could, and would have.

I wish I had it to do all over again.

Regret is mine.

And yet, there is always hope.

Now it comes from our children's spouses.

Wouldn't you know, they take their kids, our grandchildren, to church
on Sundays.

They take the time. As busy as anyone else, they make the time.

And perhaps, just perhaps, with God's blessing, a seed or two will
find a home with our children.

Finding Him is never too late.

GET UP, MY SON

I still see him as a boy climbing the oak tree in the backyard:
　　　blond hair, smiling, proud, confident.
He was the natural athlete of the family: fast, agile, good hands,
　　　excelling in baseball, basketball, and football.
A "B" student with little effort and a leader amongst his friends, he
　　　was easy to be proud of.
He was my first-born and like no other.

I don't know exactly when the drugs began, as I attributed many of
　　　the changes in him to the "terrible teens" and growing up.
Unexplainable, unacceptable changes became obvious during his first
　　　few years of high school.
This was years after his mother had terminated our marriage and left
　　　with both my boys.
In the years following they would repeatedly move from home to
　　　home, from school to school.
This would include living in quarters above a delicatessen.
In his high school sophomore year he would try out for football and
　　　fail to make the team.
Years later, I would hear from his brother that his initial tears would
　　　turn to anger and then indifference.
It was the beginning of a free-fall from which my son has yet to fully
　　　recover.

Whatever drugs he was taking, and I never found out, would induce a
　　　series of misadventures: sleeping in the bathtub, showing up
　　　late for dinner, complaining about food and then being served
　　　that same food over his head.
There was also some trouble with the police: breaking and entering,
　　　loitering, and probably more I cannot or choose not to
　　　remember.
There was also a brief stay at a psychiatric hospital – brief because he
　　　escaped, unforgettable because he found refuge in the woods
　　　behind our house.
The police would find him at an abandoned day camp and return him
　　　to the hospital.

After a few days of medication, he would be returned to his mother.

An inheritance would soon make possible a change of scenery for
      mother and first-born. They would move to an artist colony in
      Santa Fe, NM. His brother would stay behind with the
      "merged" family. Later he would graduate high school and
      then college. It was good to have him home.
New money would also serve to finance first-born's trips to a host of
      major league baseball parks and a stay in Fort Lauderdale,
      FL, where at the time the Yankees held spring training.
Houston, TX was next. Here he intended to visit a former high school
      friend.
And so, on one otherwise inconspicuous day, son grabbed his bike
      and headed for Houston, a distance of more miles than I can
      accept as doable on a bike.
As the adventure unfolds, the bike breaks down somewhere in NM
      and son turns to hitchhiking.
Either he possessed a hitchhiking gene or he quickly developed a
      knack for it, as within a week he reached Houston and located
      his friend.
Where he slept and what he ate during his interstate venture remains a
      mystery – as he never would explain.
The call from Houston came late at night.
It was the friend looking for help.
As nicely as he could, he requested that someone come get the
      "traveler" out of his house.
Our days of peace and quiet were over.
The next day second-born flew to Houston where he picked up his
      brother and returned him to his mother in NY. She had given up
on the artist colony and had returned to NY.
As I said, "our days of peace and quiet were over."

It was a sick boy who returned to NY: he had lost considerable weight, his
complexion matched the white clothes that he chose to wear, and his hair
was of such length that it made shoulder-length seem conservative.
Worst of all, he was speaking irrationally and hearing voices.

Visits to both psychiatrists and psychologists brought a diagnosis of

paranoid-schizophrenia and a series of prescribed medications,
that would calm him and muffle the voices.

Time and family would add to his improvement.

He would be invited to most all family gatherings, gain some weight,
and even shorten his more than shoulder-length hair.

Odd jobs would keep him busy and provide some ready cash.

This would allow him to participate in the family Christmas
celebrations, when he would bring gifts for all.

From both income and presents he would expand his ever-loving,
ever-growing baseball card collection. I refer to a collection
started as a boy and that today would total in number in the
thousands – all labeled and categorized.

My son had something else going for him, something I considered far
more valuable – he could draw, more specifically he could
sketch, copy a picture with remarkable accuracy.

And so for many years I requested and received as gifts sketches of
famous baseball players: Ruth, Gehrig, Cobb, W. Johnson,
Wagner, Dimaggio, Mantle , Ford.

I marveled at his talent and proudly showed off his pictures whenever
given the opportunity. Today his framed sketches are on
display in our new home.

Believing he either didn't need the prescribed medication he was
taking, or that she could replace it with herbs, his
mother stopped the medication. She would realize her
misjudgment when after only a few weeks he would
physically threaten her.

Back came the medication and things settled down once again.

They would stay that way for a decade with little change in either his
behavior or the medication received.

He would rely on his mother, brother, and family for both
entertainment and transportation. He would think nothing of
asking for a ride at any time or inviting himself anywhere.

I have to say this bothered me as somehow I felt anyone, who could
manage to travel from one state to another with no more than
a bike and a gene for hitchhiking, should be able to get
around locally by himself.

And in the back of my mind was the ever-growing feeling that most all of his good deeds came with a guaranteed return policy, meaning that a return favor was now due him, it's size determined by his need at the time.

In the beginning of the year '07, "mother love" would again rear its wishful head, and mother would take son off the prescribed medication – all of them, all overnight.

The results were not disastrous this time. There were no outbursts of violence. What came instead was lethargy – a lack of ambition, interest, and effort.

And so, since January '07 son has given up all work, all drawings, anything that would require effort.

Now his days are filled with endless hours of TV – namely the Yankees and most all other sporting events.

When I inquire as to why no job, when I expound on the merits of working, he claims his back needs rest.

Whatever ambition existed seems to have taken a sabbatical.

I receive this change in behavior with a mixed feelings of disappointment, anger, sadness, and regret.

I am disappointed because son has done little with his life and is wasting God's wonderful gift to him.

I am angry for the same reasons and also for what I see as his efforts to use his family's kindness for his own personal gain.

I am sad and regretful because I am not convinced I couldn't have done more to help him.

I am not sure of exactly what, or when, but surely more than I did.

He is and always will be my son, my first-born, and I shall always love him..

Yet I want to be as proud of him as I am of my other children, and I know not how or why I should be.

Were he physically handicapped, and I would see him making an effort at succeeding in something, I would feel pride and offer my every assistance.

But as it is and has been for so many years, with little or no effort to be seen, I can but look away and regret his indifference.

It All Matters

I would pray for God's help, but I cannot, as I have always believed
   that what must come first in any human struggle is the
   individual's effort to help his/her self.
I don't see that. I have not seen that since his childhood.
Am I asking too much from you, son?
Am I asking for more than you are capable of giving?
Forgive me if that is the case.
But I think not: I think effort can and should come from everyone.
Show me some initiative, some purpose, some determination.
Tell me of your plans for the future, your hopes and goals.
Do something worthwhile with the gift God has given you, and I
   promise you He will be there for you, as will I and all those
   who love you.
Get up, my son; there's your life to be led:
   - your dreams to be fulfilled,
   - your paths to be chosen,
   - your efforts to be realized.
Get up, my son.

ANOTHER LETTER
---- ANOTHER SON

May 5, 2006

My Dear Son,

I wrote you a letter many years ago upon graduation from college.
It was at a turning point in your life, and I wanted you to know how
      proud I was of you for your accomplishments and plans
      for the future.
I wish I had a copy of that letter now because I would send it to you
      again.
Know that I will always be proud of you son, and know of my love
      for you.

What you are experiencing now is as bad as it gets.
I know because I had a taste of it, perhaps for a different reason,
      perhaps for a similar one, and probably not as long or severe
      as yours, but for a period of time I couldn't sleep and suffered
      from anxiety attacks.
I also recall that when I was fortunate enough to fall asleep, something
      would jerk me awake as if to say, "Where do you think
      you're going?"
This might happen several times during the night until I couldn't fall
      asleep again.
I tell you this because I hear you now have a similar problem,
      and I want you to know it is not unique. It is anxiety,
      a common ailment in today's stressful environment.
Medication and several months of talking to a psychologist brought
      me back and helped me realize the reason for my anxiety.
That's the key, son, finding out the why and how.
Once aware, you can both overcome and prevent.
I thank God for the help I received and ask Him now to help you
      realize that with similar help you not only will get past this
      setback but also become stronger and more capable of dealing
      with the stresses of life. I also believe part of your recovery
      must come from you, meaning you need to make more
      time for yourself, more time to find and do your thing, and less

time doing for and pleasing others.

As your father and someone who wants the best for you,
    I ask you to believe that this setback carries with it the
    beginning of a new path in your life that you will soon take.
Whatever that is, wherever that takes you, know that without any
    doubt there is a family behind you that both loves and
    supports you.
Once as a lad when you were playing football, I asked you to get
    angry. You did, and as I recall, you then made several
    fine plays.
I ask you again now son, get angry, get aggressive.
Realize you have something new to tackle, that could bring you a
    new way of life and help you better cope with stress.
That's what you have to determine, and that's what medication and
    professional consultation and an aggressive attitude will
    bring you.
Embrace the love that is offered you and continue on with your life.
Stop worrying about what others think. Those who matter will
    understand and support you.

As a way of coping with adversity and as a means of defense,
    Grandpa would frequently rely on a crude, much over used
    expression. No, it wasn't "darn it," and it certainly wasn't
    "fiddlesticks." It was far more abusive than that and not
    easily forgotten.
Well, I still refer to his words. Once in a while I'll say them to myself.
    They help put things in a different perspective. Usually,
    however, I find that the best approach lies somewhere
    between his words and over-concern.
When you're ready, you and I will sit down and talk about whatever you
want.

I say all this with concern for you and extend to you from all your
    family much love and a speedy recovery.

Dad

DEAR SON

June 3, 2006

Dear Son,

It's raining here, and as usual on a rainy day I try to write.
My thoughts drift to you and your current struggle.
There is much I do not know, and as guessing is dangerous, I will
    leave most issues to the professionals.

Here's what I do know and feel is important for you to realize:
        your worrying about anything and everything is the worst
        thing you can do. As always, worrying solves nothing, and in
        your case it feeds the very anxiety and depression you struggle
        to overcome. I know it's easier said than done, but "done" it
        must be. Stop worrying. Cut it off. Paying tribute to a
        problem does not include worrying. It does include a
        careful examination of the facts and possible courses of action
        to be taken. It concludes with the implementation of one or
        more of those courses of action.
So let's assume you have done all that: you have examined,
        determined, and implemented to the best of your ability.
Now comes the best and easiest part, the part that helps relieve
        anxiety and allows peace of mind. You turn all your remaining
        cares and concerns over to God.
You put it in His hands.
He's quite a problem solver, and He's always there for you.
And, son, look at it this way, "If He is with you, who can be against
        you?"

Sorry if I preach, but these are the words that have both comforted
        and sustained me over the years, and, I promise, they can serve
        you as well.

I await the OK to visit.

Love,
Dad

ON THE EDGE

September 8, 2006

Why is this so difficult to write about?

Why do words come so slowly as I attempt to relate to you my son's
"fall," and his struggle to recover.

Perhaps it is because I love him as a father loves a son, and because
we are similar in many ways, and because a little of what
happened to him "knocked on my door" not so long ago.
And, therefore, I know of his pain and am reluctant to relive it.

The condition was once labeled, nervous breakdown.

Today it is more appropriately referred to as career burnout.

Either way, it is a terrifying experience.

When one is overly conscientious, when one tries to please everyone,
has trouble saying "no" to anyone, takes most everything
seriously, leaves no time for oneself, is first and foremost duty-
bound, and then applies all these behavioral patterns to his
career and achieving success with an employer who relentlessly
pressures yet for more, then one is most likely assured of that
same "knock on the door" and the stress that awaits behind it.

And stress, continuous and uncontrolled, will invariably breed serious
problems, one of which may be trouble sleeping.

If unchecked, trouble sleeping may well lead to no sleeping.

Occasional anxiety attacks will likely accompany this regression,
increasing in both frequency and intensity.

Irrational thinking follows and completes the breakdown.

All this happened to my son.

It didn't just happen. It developed over a period of years.

He would be forty-five when it would all catch up with him, and he
would take the hard fall.

He had struggled against it, believing he could and would overcome
the symptoms, all of which, at one time or another, he
suffered.

But stress and its effects would not be denied.

Self-prescribed sleep medications would fail as he would struggle

233

against the numbing effects and literally and physically
    jerk himself conscious.
At the end, he wasn't sleeping at all.
Problems became exaggerated to the point of being unrealistic.
Concerns about the uncertainty of his future would dominate his
    thoughts.
He both questioned and worried about everything.
A lack of sleep over a long period of time will do that – it will
    dominate your thoughts, exaggerate your problems, and
    challenge your very sanity.
Following his decline and unable to help him, his wife would take him
    to the hospital where much needed treatment would begin.
It took the better part of a week, but the right medication in the right
    dosage would be found, and he would at last find sleep.

High blood pressure would also be successfully treated with
    medication.
These would be the first of many steps on the road to recovery.
Once released from the hospital, he was then required to attend group
    sessions as an out-patient.
Although he hated it and felt out of place, the sessions stimulated his
    desire to get well and get out, and therefore they worked as a
    second successful step in the treatment.

It was at this time that I decided to travel north and see him.
    I was accompanied by my wife, his step-mom.
While in the hospital, he had refused to see anyone with the exception
    of his wife.
Pride will do that. He wanted no one else to see him as he was and
    where he was.
But now he was home, and we could wait no longer.

It had been a month since we had last seen him.
We had combined a college reunion weekend with a Mother's Day
    celebration with the family.
He arrived late.
You could tell immediately that something was very wrong.
He looked nervous, uncertain, and obviously had lost considerable

weight.

Most upsetting, however, were his half-closed eyes, which cried out
for help.

I regret that I didn't realize at the time how close he was to the edge.

Instead, I recommended Ambien, which he later took and fought and
which actually worsened his condition.

Now here I was again, one month later trying to help, but fearful I
would make things worse.

I would be the first of our family to see him, and I was nervous
not knowing what to expect, uncertain of what to say.

As I usually do when answers are difficult to come by, I prayed for
guidance.

His wife welcomed me at the door and led me to my son who was
standing in the kitchen, all six feet three, 225 pounds of
him.

He looked surprisingly good – a little less weight, but not too much,
and his eyes were clear and calm, and the "lost" appearance I
remembered from Mother's Day was gone. I was both relieved
and pleased.

Over lunch, he casually expressed a few of his concerns: his job,
how and why all this had happened to him, his embarrassment
at meeting with family, friends, and even neighbors.

"What do I tell them?" he said. "How do I explain what happened
when I don't know myself?"

Together his wife and I addressed his concerns, and then we did it
again emphasizing that his job was secure for as long as he
was on disability and that he had but started a third of the
possible twenty-two-week period of coverage.

We also attempted to explain the relative unimportance of what others
thought and how such misguided concern could hinder
his progress.

We tried, but I left there realizing my son needed help we could
not provide.

I was thankful that as part of the healing program he would be
meeting with professionals.

I would see him once more before returning south.

This time my wife would join me, becoming the second person
      besides his wife and son to see him. I saw that as progress.
Our meeting was short and once again over lunch.
On this visit he seemed to minimize his concerns and mask
      his problems. Perhaps pride took over and he felt his
      problems were his to solve and that to share them would
      indicate a sign of weakness. Once again, I was thankful for and
      welcomed his upcoming discussions with professionals.
Perhaps they could expose the core problem and help provide him
      with the means by which to cope and correct.
Upon leaving, it was my hope that with professional guidance my son
      would "overcome," that he would, in fact, become all the
      stronger for the experience.
I told him just that, and added that one day he would look back on
      this nightmare as a learning experience, and in the end he
      would be all the better for it.
I pray for that end each day – that my son will accept the wisdom
      of the doctors and that he will welcome the Lord
      into his heart.

Now back home, I had to rely on weekly phone conversations to
      follow his progress.
And progress he did.
He accepted visits from his Mom and brother and returned phone
      calls to the rest of the family identifying himself as the
      "wacky" one.
It was his way of breaking the tension and making the call easier for
      everyone.
Daily walks soon led to garden work and lifting weights and then
      shopping.
He continued on with the doctors, and, showing the return of his
      sense of humor, he mimed his psychologist's Indian accent.
He also complained that she only asked questions, questions he
      sought answers to.
I suggested that perhaps the answers had to come from him, and thus
      her questions.

A week later, he set a tentative date of August 7th to return to work.

When I asked him what he intended to do differently to avoid a
     similar set back, he replied, "draw a line in the sand, delegate to
     others, and consider my own needs more."

"Good," I said, "all good," and suggested he write down the specifics,
     as to how, when, and why.

Such a written list, I claimed, would serve as constant reminder.

I took his "humph" as a sign of consideration, but when I suggested
     he begin his return week with half days, he countered with the
     idea of working two to three full days for the first week,
     explaining he could get more done that way.

Something about his reply bothered me. But at the time I couldn't
     identify it.

A week later he called and confirmed his intended return date of
     August 7th.

He sounded great, like himself, and I was pleased, until he spoke of
     his need to catch up, and then I realized what had bothered me
     about his preference to initially working full days; it was the
     thought that he could get more done that way. My reply was as
     direct as I dared, telling him what he needed to realize was that
     his most important goal should be long-term, like reaching
     the minimum retirement age, still nine years off. And to reach
     that goal, he needed to better pace himself and make some
     changes in his approach to his job.

He said he knew and would work on it.

As planned, he returned to work on August 7th.

Referring to his first day back, he commented that he found the
     waters, "cold and deep," and that he felt somewhat
     overwhelmed.

Encouragingly, he broke away after a few hours and returned home.

I called again at the end of the week, which was described by him as a
     continuation of the first day.

When he told me of his effort to make up for lost time and lost sales,
     I strongly encouraged him to use the first few weeks to adjust,
     to become acclimated, and not to make sales his number one
     objective. He didn't say much, just another "humph."

The second week back showed improvement in both his attitude and approach to work.

He seemed neither depressed, nor anxious, nor did he seem overly concerned about anything.

Just as encouraging was that he delegated a few tasks to others in the office, tasks he had previously taken care of himself.

Also of importance, was that he was deliberately leaving his lap top in the office at the close of day.

Another week passed, and this time, he called me, with more good news.

- Sales increased to ten vs. the previous week's two.
- The computer received additional use as a selling tool.
- His travel schedule reflected his own needs first.

To me, that left one aspect of his recovery unaddressed.

Unfortunately, it was to me as important as any other – making time for himself, time to do something enjoyable apart from his work, his family, and his house.

He said he had not gotten around to that yet but was working on it.

As this step involved doing for himself, I took it as one that would be slow in coming.

Well, it was a week later, and I couldn't wait to call him and see if he had found and perhaps scheduled some time for himself.

I shouldn't have been surprised when he said he was still working it, that he was conscious of the need and looking around.

Fortunately, he added that he had no idea where or what to look for.

I say fortunately, because it was understandable.

How, when you have spent your entire adult life working to reach goals, working to be successful and provide for your family, how do you suddenly then apply the brakes and ask, what about me, what about my time?

If nothing else, my son is now aware of his own needs, and I truly believe he will, in time, find a way to satisfy those needs.

When I asked him who or what contributed the most to his recovery, he replied without hesitation, "the love and support of my family."

It All Matters

When I asked about God and His love, he said,
    "Oh yes, that, too. I never prayed so much in my life."

After what seemed like months and was probably weeks,
    we talked again.
He had yet to make a move for himself.
Perhaps, I was asking too much too soon.
Perhaps he needed more time to adjust.
Overall, his work went well.
Of remaining concern, however, was the anxiety he still felt from
    either many small problems at once, or a major problem at any
    time. Either situation giving rise to a sense of apprehension
    and fear.
I'd feel a whole lot better if he could just allow himself some slack
    and realize that his problems are not unique, but rather
    common in today's stressful environment and different only in
    the demands one places on him/her self.
The pursuit of perfection may well encourage success. Unfortunately,
    such an approach carries its own high price.
My son has paid that price once, and now must fight his very nature
    to prevent a reoccurrence.

It had been a month since I last heard from him,
    and I was concerned.
Unable to reach him at work, I called his home expecting to talk
    to his wife.
My son answered the phone.
Speaking slowly and with little emotion, he explained that he thought
    it best at this time to take a few days off from work.
Unmanageable stress had once again started a cycle of anxiety,
    depression, and sleep-shortened nights.
Old concerns and fears had reemerged: job security, finances, and
    what others would think.
New demands at work had neutralized his defenses.
This time I didn't hesitate. I suggested he give some thought to
    changing jobs, a move made by many of his generation.
Hell, I said, the days of working for one employer thirty or forty years,
    retiring, and receiving a pension, was a thing of the past. Today
    most everyone was on the move, constantly looking for job

improvement of one sort or another.

Maybe, just maybe, I said, he would have to do the same.

Surprisingly, he said, he had just been discussing the possibility of a
job change with his wife.

Our brief conversation ended when he passed the phone to her.

She would describe in detail his recent fall,
how he again fought the pressure and finally yielded to it.

She also confirmed their brief discussion regarding a job change.

Quite a gal, this daughter-in-law of mine, always there for him,
always by his side.

Once again she appeared to be on top of things having already had
his medication changed after a consultation with the doctor.

We agreed that a job, or even a career change, was a course of action
to be seriously considered.

This option was to be discussed by them as soon as he felt up to it.

We left it at that, with her promise to keep me updated.

My son will find his way; he is strong willed and determined.

I am as certain of this as I am of God's love.

Three weeks passed with little change in the situation.

My son remained at a loss as to what to do.

What got my attention, and what I was unaware of, was his comment
that he was tired of selling, tired of the never-ending
demand for more.

My God, how if this were true, could he possibly think about
returning to a job where his primary responsibility was to sell
and get others to sell?

With this new insight into his problem, combined with the awareness
that he was determined to reach his company's minimum
retirement age, I strongly recommended he approach his
company with the idea of a change in job responsibilities.

Any individual who has provided twenty-two years of excellence is not
someone a successful company wishes to lose;
"winners are keepers."

I added, that if it at all possible they will find a way to hold on to you.

Give them that opportunity, I pleaded.

Do not assume that it is either your current job or nothing.

Only they know your real value to them.

Son, can you hear me?

"Why?" That's what he said to me on our most recent holiday
     trip home.
It was Christmas Eve, and I had suggested the next Tuesday as a day
     for a visit and a talk.
"Why?" he said.
I couldn't believe it!
"Because I love you, and because I'm concerned about you.
That's Why.
Because maybe there are things you want to discuss.
Because maybe I can help you.
Because that's what we frequently have done in the past when things
     went astray, we talked.
And now suddenly you want to know why we should talk?"
I was hurt. I was also depressed.
For days afterwards, I moped around feeling sorry for myself. After all
     my advice, my care and attention, my insightful letters and
     carefully thought-out solutions to his problems, he says, "Why?"
After all these years of seeking advice
     and support, he now questions its value?
"Why?" you say. "My ass!" I say.
Yes, I was angry too.
And surely, it would have to be my son to break the silence that had
     now settled over us. I mean, I've got my pride.

It was almost a week later when walking my dog, Shadow, that a
     thought flashed across my mind.
It came and went so fast I had to reach back to retrieve it. Could it be
     that he, my son, wants to solve his problems himself,
     with his wife, of course, but without his over-loving, over-
     involved, over-protective father?
Had I been practicing that which I had mocked all my adult life:
     mother love?
Could his "Why?" have meant, "I appreciate and am considering your
     input, but now leave me alone and allow me to solve my own
     problems in my own time in my own way?"
I thought of our other not-so-long-ago kids.
None had been as close to me or as similar in personality and
     therefore, as easy to read.

All had been independent of my thoughts, freer of my influence, and
    had basically kept their own work-related problems to
    themselves.
Is that what the "Why?" is all about:
    a sort of Declaration of Independence,
    a message for me to back off?
I'll wait until New Year's Eve and then I'll call and check out this
    newly found theory.
I hope it proves true that "Why?" means, "Thanks for the help Dad.
    I'll take it from here."
Wow! Would that make for a Happy New Year or what?
The next day there was a message waiting for us upon our return
    from church.
It was my son wishing us a Happy New Year and requesting
    a return call.
I did just that and wasted little time in bringing up, "Why?" and giving
    him my explanation for it.
Without the slightest hesitation, he concurred with my thoughts,
    adding only that he understood and knew I meant well.
I think I underestimated my son. I know I underestimated my son.
With all his troubles and pain, he had remained too respectful to ask
    me to back off and allow him to solve his own problems.
Well, at that moment I guess you could say I felt like an ass, a
    somewhat relieved, even happy ass, but nevertheless an ass.
All my efforts to solve his problems, well intentioned as they were,
    probably exaggerated those he already had and possibly
    added more.

Just when you think you know enough to give advice, something
    happens to make you realize that mentally you are still a child,
    with a child's knowledge.
And as so many times before, you turn to Him for help, realizing that
    only He has the answers,
    only His will be done.
My son will find his way through this without me.
With God's help and guidance and his determination, he will make
    the changes necessary and will in time be all the better for it.

It All Matters

As for me, should I ever again attempt to solve another's problem,
   I will first make every effort to make sure that my advice is
   both welcomed and helpful. I will ask the individual both if
   and how I can help.
Only with encouragement that I deem sincere and with specific needs
   that I feel I can satisfy, will I attempt to be helpful. Without
   such input, I will direct my helpfulness to my own personal
   problems of which there are many.

Life is not simple, especially if it is lived fully.
Too often, it is a struggle involving not-so-simple problems, requiring
   not-so-simple solutions.

Understand, these latest gems of guidance are not set in stone.
Life is too complex.
And the only constant is change.

EPILOGUE

It is nearly six months later.

My son has just recently gone back to work – same company, similar
job, but fewer demands.

He is still apprehensive and continues to receive both medication and
counseling.

I hesitate to call; I've interfered enough.

Yet, I need to know how he's doing.

I call. There is only the indifference of a recorded message.

I black out negative thoughts and decide to call back later.

Before I can do that, his wife returns my call.

In her words, "Everything is OK. He remains somewhat nervous and
apprehensive, but is taking it one day at a time."

Best of all, I learned that he is most comfortable selling and despite
his fears to the contrary, it has all come back to him.

Yes, everything will be OK.

It is in His hands.

It All Matters
IN HIS HANDS

It began a few years ago.
I was trying to go to sleep.
My favorite position for accomplishing that sometimes elusive state
   is lying on my left side.
I don't know why either, but any other position is not as comfortable.
So this one night in the spring of the year, I was in that favorite
   position awaiting sleep when I heard it – tap, tap, tap, tap.
I would liken the noise to the clicking together of one's front teeth.
It sounded pretty much like that, only this tapping or clicking came
   from my chest as I exhaled and only when lying on my
   left side.
To fall asleep, I had no choice but to change sides.
I mean, how do you go to sleep when your chest is playing taps?

A few days later the noise disappeared, and I attributed the symptom
   to some kind of allergy.
Everyone else seemed to have an allergy of sort, so why shouldn't I?
Over the next year the tapping would come and go.
It didn't matter what time of the year; the taps would visit for a night
   or so and then leave.
And as always, my solution would be to turn onto the right side.
Damn allergies!

After a year or so of the on-again, off-again taps at a semi-annual
   checkup, I casually mentioned the condition to my physician.
   Doc kind of stared at me for what seemed like a few minutes
   and then listened to my breathing.
Hearing nothing unusual, he nevertheless suggested I have
   an X-ray taken.
In his words, "Just to be sure everything is OK."
I wasn't really too concerned at the time. You know how doctors tend
   to overreact to symptoms.
Two days later, and with an appointment, I strutted into an X-ray
   room, flexed what remained of my chest muscles and had the
   pictures taken.
No big deal!

The very next morning the doctor's head nurse called and calmly
informed me that the X-rays showed a "spot" on the upper
portion of my left lung.
The recommendation of my doctor was to have a CT scan taken.
"You can't be too careful with something like this," again his words.
The confidence that had been mine suddenly went elsewhere.
It was difficult to keep negative thoughts away, like the
big "C" for one – a very big deal!
And so heeding my doctor's advice, I was off to the CT scan room.
No strutting this time. No flexing. Just a slightly elevated heart rate.
I did as requested, went home and awaited the results.
Again the head nurse called, again in the a.m.
The CT scan confirmed the spot, but once again did not provide
definite identification.
It showed a small area, about an inch long, of a different color than
the neighboring area.
The doctor now recommended a PET scan; supposedly a step above
the MRI, whatever that meant.

With four days to wait, I had more than enough time to think
things over.
What eventually came to mind was the advice I had given to my son,
who at this same time was struggling to overcome problems
of his own.
In one of my letters to him, I had suggested he place his concerns
in God's hands, that he should do whatever he could to solve
a problem, any problem, and then turn it over to God.
Those were my words to my son.
Now I repeated them to myself.
It took a while and more than a few repetitions, but the words did
bring comfort .
That doesn't mean I was no longer concerned and didn't on occasion
allow negative thoughts to challenge, but by putting it all in
His hands, I found the strength I needed to cope.
Yet, I could not help but wonder if the real test was yet to come,
that test being the strength of my faith. It was one thing to
find consolation through faith when the prognosis was in doubt,
but what if the prognosis were life-threatening?

It All Matters

What then?

Would my faith sustain me then?

It was a question I could not truthfully answer.

Yet, somehow, I felt strangely confident..

The PET scan was long, but the waiting for it was even longer.

We, my wife and I, arrived on time for a 4:00 p.m. appointment.

The test was concluded at 7:30 p.m..

There was no pain, just the boredom and discomfort that
        accompanies hours of sitting and waiting.

The test itself was taken in a trailer, that might also have served
        as a freezer.

A nurse shot some radioactive fluid into me, and then after forty-five
        minutes of fighting frost bite and waiting for the isotopes
        to isolate the problem, she moved me to another area where
        I was nearly entombed in a cylindrical like object that might
        well have come from outer space.

The X-ray took 20 minutes during which time the nurse instructed me
        not to move.

What the nurse didn't know, and I never thought to tell her, was that
        I suffer from RLS, restless leg syndrome.

At any given time, and for no medically explainable reason, my legs
        will twitch, twinge, or spasm, or feel like some unwanted guest
        is crawling around beneath my skin; temporary relief coming
        only from moving, massaging, or when all else fails, smashing
        the calf of my leg with my fist.

Although certainly an attention getter, this last course of action is not
        recommended by most professionals as a beneficial treatment
        for RLS.

Anyway, to not move is to ask the impossible.

I did the best I could and went so far as to create my own
        diversionary pain by pinching whatever part of my body the
        entombment would allow.

Somehow, I thought the pain of a pinch would neutralize the
        annoyance of a twitch.

I thought wrong and ended up with a body full of welts and a
        twitching calf muscle.

Some consolation did come knowing that if a double image did appear
        on the PET scan, it might well have been the result of a twitch.

The nurse promised to call with the results in a few days.

Well, a few days are up, and I sit here awaiting the call.
I'll wait until 3:00 p.m. and, if I haven't heard by then, I'll call the
     doctor's office.
I lasted until 2:30 p.m. and then called.
After five minutes of "hanging on" and listening to my heart attempt
     to leave my body, the nurse informed me of the results of the
     test. The decision was a no decision.
They, the doctors, could still not identify the spot, describing it only
     as a "nodular density" of a different color than the lung.
But they were unable to explain or identify it.
X-rays, CT scan, PET scan, weeks of waiting and concern, and
     nothing, no decision.
I felt like a pugilist who, after twelve struggling rounds, was awarded a
     "no decision."
Better than losing, no doubt, but still not winning.
And yet I was also relieved, as the diagnosis could have been far worse.
The same doctors with no answer now recommended a second CT
     scan, a "rematch," if you will, in six months, the purpose of
     which to reveal any change in the spot.
Yes, I'll do it again in six months. I need a decision, and no change in
     the spot would give me one, a win.

Once again, I call on Him.
I put myself in His hands.
I believe in Him, and believing makes the journey easier.
And best of all, believing is a choice open to all, a highway
     to accepting life's challenges with strength
     and peace of mind.
I think of my mother and kneel beside my bed.
I give thanks to God for His many blessings.
I pray my faith in Him will ever grow.

It is six months later.
I have been relatively well and attribute my recent back spasms to an
     over zealous pursuit of the perfect golf swing, and the recent
     weeks of sniffling, coughing, and chest tapping to the change

in weather and my annual pre-winter cold.
Thankfully, months of growing anxiety will soon end, as I await the
        results of my second CT scan.
I tell myself there is nothing more I can do.
What is meant to be will be by His will.

The phone rings.
It is the nurse; the same nurse who first advised me of the spot on my
        lung some six months ago.
Her voice is upbeat almost cheerful, indicating an omen of good news.
She tells me the radiologist can see no change in the nodule, and
        describes it as probable scar tissue caused by either pneumonia
        or smoking.
To be safe, the doctor recommends a series of additional CT scans,
        to be taken six months apart.
I confirm what I consider to be good news, speaking slowly and
        repeating the nurse's words aloud.
I thank her and say goodbye.
Slowly, I return the phone to its receiver, realizing the importance of
        the news.
I bow my head.
A tear gains its freedom.
I search for the right words.
None seem appropriate.
I can but whisper, "Thank you, dear Lord."
I can but believe in Him, that He is there for all who believe and call
        on Him.

Then, as if slapped with the backhand of doubt, old uncertainties
      return.
I ask myself, "What if the prognosis were different, what if the
      prognosis were life-threatening? What then?"
How would I receive that news?
Would I then accept my fate as His will?
Would I continue to embrace the words,
      "What is meant to be, will be by His will?"
Would my faith sustain me then?
Again, I feel strangely confident.
Yet, I cannot, in truth, answer these questions, not now, perhaps
      someday under different circumstances, but not now.
Now is for giving thanks.
Now is for celebrating life, for living and loving, for experiencing
      and challenging, for making new friends and renewing
      old relationships.
And above all, now is for using the time granted and the gifts given
      to better serve Him by sharing His gift with others.

Maybe I'll try writing another book, and maybe you'll try reading it.
Or, maybe you'll try writing a book, and maybe I'll try reading it.
And that's all good, not necessarily the book, but the concept; because
      in either case we're doing as He would have us do, we're
      sharing His gift with others.

By God, I think I'm becoming an optimist.
Well, you believe in miracles, don't you?
Believing is a wondrous thing.
Believing in Him is most wondrous of all.
And could it just be that this wondrous belief in Him, this faith begins
      when we first allow, then welcome Him into our hearts and minds,
      and grows as we turn to him for repeated guidance and resolution,
      for forgiveness and thanks?
Could that be the stages of faith's journey?
I rather think so.

It All Matters
EPILOGUE

As I waited for the results of my most recent CT scan and the last in a
series of three, I couldn't help but reflect on its importance.
I mean, we're talking lungs here, my lungs.
Three days had passed since the test and so I called my good luck
nurse, Lyda, for the results.
She read the radiologist's report to me – STABLE, NO CHANGE IN
MODULE – REPEAT CT SCAN IN ONE YEAR.
What a wonderful feeling! Like sunshine had just burst through some
dark, ominous clouds.

I went to my prayer spot beside the bed and noticed that there were
knee prints in the carpet.
Once again I settled in to give thanks.
I could tell from the fit that they were definitely my prints.
It's important to me to be original when I give thanks, but how many
ways can you say, thank you?
I thought of nodding my head up and down as I had years ago in
church or giving a thumbs-up for approval, but then I thought
better of the idea and simply said, "Thank you Lord for
watching over me."
Sometimes simplest is best, and as it comes so naturally to me, I
frequently rely on its usage.
And I'm sure the carpet welcomes its new usage; better to receive knee
with gentle prayer than foot with dirty shoe. – future Chinese proverb.

God has a sense of humor, right?
I think I'll add that wish to my prayer list.

ABOUT THE AUTHOR

The author was born in Flushing, NY during the depression.
The hospital bill was $80. His father said it was a rip off.
 Raised in Jackson Heights and Forest Hills, Queens, NY.
A graduate of Rutgers University of New Jersey, where college football
   began in 1869, and where today, after decades of frustration, a
   nationally top ranked team and Bowl winner takes the field. And
   where in 2007, for the first time ever, a group of women athletes
   joined together to bring the Rutgers basketball team to the NCAA
   finals.
Served in the army for two years at Fort Bliss, Texas as an instructor and
   then spent the next 33 years selling and wondering why he left
   the service.
Now retired, he resides in a golfing community in Calabash, NC,
   where he applies what's left of his body to golf and what's left of
   his mind to writing.
Loves and enjoys his wife, Elaine, who forever spoils him, and his six
   children and their families, all of whom do their utmost to accept
   this "salty old dog."

Order this book online at www.trafford.com/07-0170
or email orders@trafford.com

Most Trafford titles are also available at major online book retailers.

Note for Librarians: A cataloguing record for this book is available from Library
and Archives Canada at www.collectionscanada.ca/amicus/index-e.html

Printed in Victoria, BC, Canada.

ISBN: 978-1-4251-1708-5

*We at Trafford believe that it is the responsibility of us all, as both individuals
and corporations, to make choices that are environmentally and socially sound.
You, in turn, are supporting this responsible conduct each time you purchase a
Trafford book, or make use of our publishing services. To find out how you are
helping, please visit www.trafford.com/responsiblepublishing.html*

*Our mission is to efficiently provide the world's finest, most comprehensive
book publishing service, enabling every author to experience success.
To find out how to publish your book, your way, and have it available
worldwide, visit us online at www.trafford.com/10510*

 www.trafford.com

North America & international
toll-free: 1 888 232 4444 (USA & Canada)
phone: 250 383 6864 ♦ fax: 250 383 6804 ♦ email: info@trafford.com

The United Kingdom & Europe
phone: +44 (0)1865 722 113 ♦ local rate: 0845 230 9601
facsimile: +44 (0)1865 722 868 ♦ email: info.uk@trafford.com

10 9 8 7 6 5 4 3 2

ISBN 142511708-2